Good Housekeeping
ONE DISH!

Oven-Baked Drumsticks and Dipping Veggies (page 121)

Good Housekeeping

ONE DISH!

90 IRRESISTIBLY EASY DINNERS THAT ARE READY WHEN YOU ARE

HEARST BOOKS
New York

HEARST BOOKS
New York

An Imprint of Sterling Publishing
387 Park Avenue South
New York, NY 10016

ISBN 978-1-61837-086-0

GOOD HOUSEKEEPING
Rosemary Ellis
EDITOR IN CHIEF

Courtney Murphy
CREATIVE DIRECTOR

Susan Westmoreland
FOOD DIRECTOR

Samantha B. Cassetty, M.S., R.D.
NUTRITION DIRECTOR

Sharon Franke
**KITCHEN APPLIANCES AND FOOD
TECHNOLOGY DIRECTOR**

BOOK DESIGN: Memo Productions
PROJECT EDITOR: Sarah Scheffel
Photography Credits on page 158

The Good Housekeeping Cookbook Seal
guarantees that the recipes in this cookbook
meet the strict standards of the Good
Housekeeping Research Institute. The Institute
has been a source of reliable information and
a consumer advocate since 1900, and established
its seal of approval in 1909. Every recipe has
been triple-tested for ease, reliability, and
great taste.

Distributed in Canada by Sterling Publishing
c/o Canadian Manda Group, 165 Dufferin Street
Toronto, Ontario, Canada M6K 3H6

Distributed in the United Kingdom by
GMC Distribution Services
Castle Place, 166 High Street, Lewes, East Sussex,
England BN7 1XU

Distributed in Australia by Capricorn Link
(Australia) Pty. Ltd.
P.O. Box 704, Windsor, NSW 2756, Australia

For information about custom editions,
special sales, and premium and corporate
purchases, please contact Sterling Special
Sales at 800-805-5489 or
specialsales@sterlingpublishing.com.

Manufactured in China

2   4   6   8   10   9   7   5   3   1

www.sterlingpublishing.com

CONTENTS

A Trio of Tartines (page 144)

FOREWORD

How often do you say, "I think I'll make a one-dish dinner tonight"? I never do, but I'm often trying to take the shortest real-food path to weeknight dinner, so I naturally gravitate toward pastas, stir-fries, hearty soups, and main-dish salads—aka one-dish meals.

In this volume, we've collected 90 of *Good Housekeeping's* all-time favorites, so you're sure to find an easy and irresistible one-dish dinner to tempt you any night of the week. In the introduction, you'll find advice on stocking your pantry, meal prep shortcuts, and how to freeze (and reheat) leftovers with ease—along with tips that'll help you make one-dish magic in a nonstick skillet or slow cooker.

Soups and stews like Spicy Turkey Chili and Shrimp and Sausage Gumbo are one-pot perfection. Just slice up the ingredients, toss them in a pot, and you'll have a wholesome meal for your family at the end of a long day. Or serve up some comfort with one of our soul-satisfying casseroles. What could be more appealing than breaking the crust of a potpie brimming with turkey, carrots, and peas in a creamy sauce? Or digging into a creamy polenta and sausage casserole?

If you're looking for speed, you'll love our stir-fries and skillet suppers. In one pan, you can toss together favorites like Cashew Chicken Stir-Fry or Smothered Pork Chops; most can be prepared in 30 minutes—or less! In warmer weather, assemble one of our salads or sandwiches—Shrimp and Tomato Summer Salad is light and refreshing, while hearty sandwiches like Philly Cheese Steaks will satisfy even the most robust appetite.

Our goal is to make your life easier: By plotting dinners in a single pot or pan, we help you streamline menu planning, shopping, cooking, and cleanup. So, open to any page of *Good Housekeeping One Dish!* and cook up a delicious dinner that's ready when you are.

SUSAN WESTMORELAND
Food Director, *Good Housekeeping*

INTRODUCTION

One-dish meals are all about getting dinner on the table with ease. Whether you're making one of our stir-fries in a nonstick skillet, soup or stew in a slow cooker, or using the oven to bake a casserole or make a succulent roast, the tips that follow will help you get the job done efficiently—and with delicious results!

STOCK YOUR PANTRY

You'll want to keep these convenience foods on hand.

• **Canned beans:** From kidney beans to cannellini, you'll want a selection on hand for soups, stews, and even sandwiches like Falafel and Pinto-Bean Burgers (pages 148 and 149).

• **Canned chicken, beef, and vegetable broths:** The basis for most soups, stews, and slow-cooker dinners, they're also used in dishes like Smothered Pork Chops (page 54). Try the low-sodium versions.

• **Canned tomatoes, tomato paste:** Essential to many pastas and casseroles, including Polenta and Sausage Casserole (page 96).

• **Jarred salsa:** Beyond its obvious use as a dip, we call for it in cozy dishes like Tamale Pie (page 92). Mild, medium, or hot—you decide.

• **Dried pasta:** Pasta is a go-to dinner in most households, so stock up on your favorite shapes, including whole-wheat options.

• **Rice:** For ease, stock up on fast-cooking products like long-grain white rice and precooked packages of brown rice—so convenient when you want to make Stir-Fried Steak and Vegetables (page 51).

• **Cornmeal:** If this isn't a staple in your pantry it should be. You'll need it for Chili Potpie with Biscuit Crust (page 88).

SHORTCUTS TO MEAL PREPARATION

• Choose lean cuts of meat, such as chicken breasts, which will cook faster than fattier cuts. Save tougher cuts of red meat, such as a pork shoulder-blade roast, for the slow cooker.

• Put water on to boil or preheat the oven as soon as you get home. Meanwhile, you can gather your ingredients, brown meat, or sauté onions, according to the recipe's requirements.

• If you are using ground beef or turkey in a recipe, brown it the previous evening, then let it cool, bag it, and refrigerate.

• Cook enough for two meals and turn the leftovers into different dishes later in the week. For example, the leftovers from a generous pot of chili can be used to make tacos and nachos—or as a great baked potato topping.

• Freeze leftovers in individual servings, and you'll have a stockpile of quick and tasty meals whenever you want.

SAFE NONSTICK COOKING

Easy to clean and very popular, nonstick skillets make preparing one-dish meals a breeze. Just follow these cooking guidelines to keep your pans safe and in good shape.

1. Never preheat an empty nonstick pan, even one with oil in it.

2. Don't cook over high heat. Most nonstick manufacturers now advise consumers not to go above medium. (The coating on nonstick pans may begin to break down at temperatures above 500°F.)

3. Ventilate your kitchen. As with all stovetop cooking, turn on the exhaust fan to help clear away any fumes.

4. Don't broil or sear meats in a nonstick pan. Those techniques require temperatures above what nonstick can usually handle.

5. Choose a heavier nonstick pan. Lightweight pans generally heat up fastest; heavier cookware is worth the extra money.

6. Avoid scratching or chipping the pan. Use wooden spoons for stirring, don't use steel wool for cleaning, and don't stack the pans when you store them. (If you do, place a paper towel between them.)

SLOW-COOKER SUCCESS

The slow cooker allows you to prepare flavorful soups and stews and meltingly tender meat with a minimum of effort, all in a single pot. Here are tips to ensure that you get the most out of your slow cooker.

1. Prep the night before, and all you'll need to do in the morning is toss your ingredients into the slow-cooker bowl and flip the switch. (Measure ingredients, cut veggies, and trim fat from meats, then refrigerate components separately in bowls or storage bags so, for instance, the acid in wine doesn't change the texture of the meat.)

2. Less tender cuts of meat and poultry—such as pork and lamb shoulder, chuck roast, beef brisket, and poultry legs—are best suited for slow cooking. Skim fat from cooking liquid when done. (Fish and other seafood aren't good candidates unless they are added in the last hour of cooking.)

3. Slow cooking tends to intensify flavorful spices and seasonings such as chili powder and garlic, so use them conservatively. Dried herbs may lessen in flavor, so adjust seasonings by stirring in a little more at the end of cooking. When using fresh herbs, save some to toss in at the last minute for freshness and color.

4. For richer flavor in stews, sprinkle meat and poultry with flour and brown in skillet before slow cooking. (Scrape up browned bits in skillet and add to the pot to help thicken sauce and enhance flavor.)

5. Resist the urge to take the lid off and stir ingredients; the pot will lose valuable heat.

FREEZE (AND REHEAT) WITH EASE

Many of the soups, stews, casseroles, and savory pies in this book are perfect one-dish candidates for freezing. Make two and freeze one for double-duty dinners you can enjoy on a busy weeknight.

To Freeze

Before freezing, refrigerate soups or stews for 30 minutes; casseroles need 30 minutes at room temperature plus 30 minutes in the fridge. Wrap casseroles tightly in foil or plastic wrap. Seal soups and stews in zip-tight plastic bags or freezer containers (usually thicker plastic). To maximize space, stack bags horizontally until frozen, then store upright. Or line your baking dish with heavy-duty greased foil before making the casserole; once the meal is frozen solid, remove the frozen food and transfer it to a large resealable plastic bag.

To Thaw

Soups, Stews, and Chilis: Place frozen food, still sealed in a plastic bag, in a bowl or sink of hot water for five to ten minutes or until it can be broken into pieces. If the food is in a sealed freezer-weight container, leave it in hot water until the food separates from its sides. Open

the bag or container; invert contents into a saucepan (for stovetop heating) or into a microwave-safe bowl.

Casseroles and Savory Pies: At least 24 hours but no more than two days before reheating, refrigerate the frozen casserole to thaw it slightly. If the casserole was frozen in a foil-lined baking dish and then removed from the dish for storage, unwrap it and slip it back into the baking dish to thaw.

To Reheat

On the Stovetop: To reheat soups, stews, and chilis, add ¼ to ½ cup water to the saucepan to prevent scorching. Cover and heat to boiling over medium heat, then boil 1 minute to be sure it's fully heated; stir frequently throughout.

In a Conventional Oven: To reheat casseroles, unwrap the frozen item and place in the baking dish it was made in; loosely cover casserole with foil and bake about 1 hour, then uncover and bake 20 to 30 minutes longer or until the center of the casserole reaches 160°F on an instant-read thermometer.

In a Microwave: Put soups, stews, and chilis in a microwave-safe bowl and cover with waxed paper or vented plastic wrap. Heat in microwave about 10 minutes, first on Low (30%) until ice crystals are gone, then on High 5 to 15 minutes longer, until the soup, stew, or chili is heated through. Note: Do not allow plastic wrap to touch food during microwaving because it may melt.

Don't remove the carousel in your microwave to accommodate large casseroles—a microwave that rotates food won't do its job without turning. Unwrap the casserole; cover the top of the microwave-safe dish with waxed paper or plastic wrap and turn back a corner to vent. Heat in the microwave about 30 minutes on Low (30%) until ice crystals are gone and you can easily insert a knife into center of casserole. Then heat on High 5 to 15 minutes longer, until food is heated through, and the internal temperature of the casserole is 160°F.

Layered Three-Bean Casserole (page 117)

SOUPS & STEWS

Here we offer a sampling of one-pot perfection: Choose from familiar favorites like Chicken and Rosemary Dumplings and Beef and Barley Stew, or sample international classics like Creamy Italian White-Bean Soup and Mediterranean Seafood Stew. And, of course, chili: a trio of recipes featuring beef, ground turkey, and three beans and veggies. Soups and stews often taste even better the next day, which means leftovers are sure to satisfy.

KEY TO ICONS

⊙ 30 minutes or less   ♥ Heart healthy   ☺ Low calorie   ▭ Make ahead   ◰ Slow cooker

Shrimp and Sausage Gumbo (page 34)

BEEF BOURGUIGNON

Americans have come to love this French classic. It originated in the Burgundy region, which is renowned for the wonderful wine that is the basis for this robust stew. Serve with boiled potatoes or chunks of crusty French bread. See "Browning and Braising Basics," opposite, for tips.

ACTIVE TIME: 30 MINUTES · TOTAL TIME: 3 HOURS 15 MINUTES
MAKES: 6 MAIN-DISH SERVINGS

2   SLICES BACON, CHOPPED

2   POUNDS LEAN BONELESS BEEF CHUCK, TRIMMED AND CUT INTO 1½-INCH PIECES

2   TEASPOONS VEGETABLE OIL

1   LARGE ONION (12 OUNCES), CHOPPED

2   CARROTS, PEELED AND CHOPPED

2   GARLIC CLOVES, FINELY CHOPPED

2   TABLESPOONS ALL-PURPOSE FLOUR

2   TEASPOONS TOMATO PASTE

2   CUPS DRY RED WINE, PREFERABLY BURGUNDY

½   BAY LEAF

1   TEASPOON PLUS PINCH SALT

¼   TEASPOON PLUS PINCH GROUND BLACK PEPPER

1   POUND SMALL WHITE ONIONS, PEELED

3   TABLESPOONS BUTTER OR MARGARINE

1   TEASPOON SUGAR

1   CUP WATER

1   POUND MUSHROOMS, TRIMMED AND CUT INTO QUARTERS IF LARGE

1   In nonreactive 5-quart Dutch oven, cook bacon over medium heat until just beginning to brown. With slotted spoon, transfer bacon to medium bowl, leaving bacon drippings in pan.

2   Pat beef dry with paper towels. Add 1 teaspoon oil to bacon drippings in Dutch oven and increase heat to medium-high. Add beef, in batches, to bacon drippings and cook until well browned, using slotted spoon to transfer beef as it is browned to bowl with bacon. Add remaining 1 teaspoon oil if beef begins to stick to pan.

3   Reduce heat to medium. Add chopped onion, carrots, and garlic to Dutch oven; cook until onion and carrots are tender, about 8 minutes. Stir in flour; cook 1 minute. Stir in tomato paste; cook 1 minute. Add wine, bay leaf, 1 teaspoon salt, and ¼ teaspoon pepper, stirring until browned bits are loosened. Return beef and bacon to Dutch oven; heat to boiling. Reduce heat; cover and simmer until beef is very tender, about 1 hour 30 minutes. Remove bay leaf. Skim and discard fat.

BROWNING AND BRAISING BASICS

Mastering these techniques is essential to achieving rich, succulent meat stews.

- Make sure the pan and oil are very hot before adding the meat in small batches (a pound or less at a time). Overcrowding the pan will steam the meat instead of allowing it to brown.

- Allow the meat to brown on all sides, caramelizing the proteins and sugars. (Reduce the heat if the bits of meat clinging to the bottom of the pan begin to burn.)

- Add liquid to the meat in the pan only after browning is complete, and heat to boiling, scraping the bottom of the pan with a spoon to release the browned bits. (This process is known as deglazing.)

- Cover the pan and braise the mixture over lower heat on the stovetop or at a moderate temperature (325° to 350°F) in the oven, according to recipe instructions. Do not allow the stew to boil—the meat will toughen and dry out.

- When the meat is tender and fully braised, the tines of a fork will slip easily in and out of the pieces.

4 Meanwhile, in 10-inch skillet, combine small white onions, 1 tablespoon butter, sugar, and water. Heat to boiling; cover and simmer until onions are just tender, about 10 minutes. Remove cover and cook over medium-high heat, swirling pan occasionally, until water has evaporated and onions are golden. Transfer to bowl; keep warm.

5 In same skillet, melt remaining 2 tablespoons butter over medium-high heat. Add mushrooms and remaining pinch each salt and pepper; cook, stirring, until mushrooms are tender and liquid has evaporated. Stir onions and mushrooms into stew.

EACH SERVING: About 415 calories | 33g protein | 20g carbohydrate | 23g total fat (9g saturated) | 116mg cholesterol | 261mg sodium

SUPER BOWL CHILI

Our recipe for Texas-style chili contains small *chunks* of beef rather than ground. The classic version doesn't contain beans, but we replaced a portion of the meat with red kidney beans to cut some fat. Serve with corn bread or tortilla chips.

ACTIVE TIME: 30 MINUTES · TOTAL TIME: 2 HOURS 40 MINUTES

MAKES: 14 CUPS OR 12 MAIN-DISH SERVINGS

2	TABLESPOONS OLIVE OIL	2	CANS (28 OUNCES EACH) WHOLE TOMATOES IN PUREE
2	POUNDS BONELESS BEEF FOR STEW, CUT INTO ½-INCH CHUNKS	1	CAN (6 OUNCES) TOMATO PASTE
4	GARLIC CLOVES, CRUSHED WITH GARLIC PRESS	¼	CUP SUGAR
		2	TEASPOONS SALT
2	RED PEPPERS, CUT INTO ½-INCH PIECES	2	TEASPOONS DRIED OREGANO
2	JALAPEÑO CHILES, SEEDED AND MINCED	2	CUPS WATER
1	LARGE ONION, CHOPPED	2	CANS (15 TO 19 OUNCES EACH) RED KIDNEY BEANS, RINSED AND DRAINED
⅓	CUP CHILI POWDER		

1 In 8-quart saucepot or Dutch oven, heat 1 teaspoon oil over high heat until hot. Add one-third of beef and cook until browned on all sides and liquid evaporates, 6 to 8 minutes, stirring often. With slotted spoon, transfer beef to bowl. Repeat with remaining beef, using 1 teaspoon oil per batch; set beef aside.

2 Add remaining 1 tablespoon oil to drippings in saucepot and heat over medium-high heat until hot. Stir in garlic, red peppers, jalapeños, and onion; cook until vegetables are tender, about 10 minutes, stirring occasionally. Stir in chili powder; cook 1 minute.

3 Return beef to saucepot. Stir in tomatoes with their puree, tomato paste, sugar, salt, oregano, and water, breaking up tomatoes with side of spoon; heat to boiling over high heat. Reduce heat to low; cover and simmer 1 hour and 30 minutes. Stir in beans and cook 10 to 30 minutes longer or until meat is fork-tender, stirring occasionally.

EACH SERVING: ABOUT 275 CALORIES | 25G PROTEIN | 30G CARBOHYDRATE | 7G TOTAL FAT (2G SATURATED) | 36MG CHOLESTEROL | 1,115MG SODIUM ☺ ▭

BEEF AND BARLEY STEW

Nutty-tasting barley is a delicious change from noodles in this meaty stew. What's more, barley is rich in fiber, B vitamins, and minerals. Serve with a salad to round out the meal.

ACTIVE TIME: 45 MINUTES · TOTAL TIME: 3 HOURS 15 MINUTES

MAKES: 16 CUPS OR 8 MAIN-DISH SERVINGS

1   TABLESPOON PLUS 4 TEASPOONS VEGETABLE OIL

3   STALKS CELERY, CHOPPED

1   LARGE ONION, CHOPPED

1½ POUNDS BONELESS BEEF CHUCK, CUT INTO ½-INCH PIECES

½   TEASPOON SALT

2   CANS (13¾ TO 14½ OUNCES EACH) BEEF BROTH

1   CAN (14½ OUNCES) DICED TOMATOES

6   CUPS WATER

1   CUP PEARL BARLEY

5   CARROTS (12 OUNCES), PEELED AND CUT CROSSWISE INTO ¼-INCH-THICK SLICES

5   PARSNIPS (12 OUNCES), PEELED AND CUT CROSSWISE INTO ¼-INCH-THICK SLICES

2   TURNIPS (8 OUNCES), PEELED AND CUT INTO 1-INCH PIECES

3   STRIPS (3" BY 1" EACH) ORANGE PEEL

PINCH GROUND CLOVES

1   In 8-quart Dutch oven, heat 1 tablespoon oil over medium-high heat until hot. Add celery and onion and cook until tender and golden, about 10 minutes, stirring occasionally; transfer vegetables to bowl.

2   Pat beef dry with paper towels. In same Dutch oven, heat 2 teaspoons oil over high heat until hot. Add half of beef and cook until browned on all sides. Remove to plate. Repeat with the remaining 2 teaspoons oil and beef.

3   Return beef to Dutch oven. Stir in salt, celery mixture, broth, tomatoes with their juice, and water; heat to boiling over high heat. Reduce heat to low; cover and simmer 1 hour.

4   Add barley, carrots, parsnips, turnips, orange peel, and cloves; heat to boiling over high heat. Reduce heat to low; cover and simmer 50 to 60 minutes or until beef, barley, and vegetables are tender.

EACH SERVING: ABOUT 320 CALORIES | 25G PROTEIN | 36G CARBOHYDRATE | 9G TOTAL FAT (3G SATURATED) | 41MG CHOLESTEROL | 740MG SODIUM ☺ 🍲

LATIN AMERICAN PORK STEW

Pork, black beans, cilantro, and sweet potatoes give this dish authentic Latino flavor.

ACTIVE TIME: 30 MINUTES · **TOTAL TIME:** 2 HOURS
MAKES: 10 CUPS OR 8 MAIN-DISH SERVINGS

2 TEASPOONS OLIVE OIL	½ TEASPOON GROUND CORIANDER
2 POUNDS BONELESS PORK LOIN, CUT INTO 1-INCH PIECES	¼ TEASPOON CAYENNE (GROUND RED) PEPPER
1 LARGE ONION, CHOPPED	2 CUPS WATER
4 GARLIC CLOVES, MINCED	3 MEDIUM SWEET POTATOES (1½ POUNDS), PEELED AND CUT INTO ½-INCH CHUNKS
1 CAN (14½ OUNCES) DICED TOMATOES	
1 CUP LOOSELY PACKED FRESH CILANTRO LEAVES AND STEMS, CHOPPED	2 CANS (15 TO 19 OUNCES EACH) BLACK BEANS, RINSED AND DRAINED
1 TEASPOON GROUND CUMIN	
¾ TEASPOON SALT	

1 Preheat oven to 350°F. In nonstick 5-quart Dutch oven, heat oil over medium heat. Add pork in batches and cook until lightly browned, 6 to 8 minutes per batch. Transfer pork to medium bowl.

2 Reduce heat to medium. In drippings in pot, cook onion until tender, about 10 minutes, stirring frequently. Add garlic and cook 1 minute longer.

3 Add tomatoes with their juice, cilantro, cumin, salt, coriander, cayenne, and water; heat to boiling over medium-high heat. Stir in pork; cover Dutch oven and bake 30 minutes.

4 Stir in sweet potatoes; cover and bake 40 minutes longer or until meat and sweet potatoes are very tender. Stir in black beans; cover and bake 15 minutes or until heated through.

EACH SERVING: ABOUT 340 CALORIES | 36G PROTEIN | 36G CARBOHYDRATE | 9G TOTAL FAT (3G SATURATED) | 58MG CHOLESTEROL | 735MG SODIUM ☺ 🍴

LAMB AND ROOT VEGETABLE TAGINE

Tagine, a traditional stew from North Africa, is known for its combination of sweet and salty ingredients. In this tender slow-cooker version, we include dried apricots, lamb, and heaps of root vegetables.

ACTIVE TIME: 30 MINUTES · SLOW-COOK TIME: 8 HOURS ON LOW
MAKES: 10 MAIN-DISH SERVINGS

1   TABLESPOON VEGETABLE OIL

4   POUNDS WELL-TRIMMED LEG OF LAMB, DEBONED, CUT INTO 1-INCH PIECES

½   TEASPOON SALT

1¾ CUPS CHICKEN BROTH

1   MEDIUM ONION, CHOPPED

2   GARLIC CLOVES, THINLY SLICED

1   POUND SWEET POTATOES (2 MEDIUM), PEELED AND CUT INTO 1-INCH PIECES

1   POUND PARSNIPS (6 MEDIUM), PEELED AND CUT INTO 1-INCH PIECES

½   CUP DRIED APRICOTS, EACH CUT IN HALF

2   TEASPOONS GROUND CORIANDER

2   TEASPOONS GROUND CUMIN

½   TEASPOON GROUND CINNAMON

2   CUPS PLAIN COUSCOUS

¾   CUP PITTED GREEN OLIVES, CHOPPED

FRESH CILANTRO LEAVES FOR GARNISH

1   In 12-inch skillet, heat oil over medium-high heat until very hot. Sprinkle lamb with salt. Add lamb to skillet in 3 batches and cook, stirring occasionally and adding more oil if necessary, until lamb is browned on all sides, 5 to 6 minutes per batch. With slotted spoon, transfer lamb to medium bowl when browned.

2   After lamb is browned, add broth to skillet and heat to boiling over high heat, stirring to loosen browned bits. Boil 1 minute.

3   Meanwhile, in 6- to 6½-quart slow-cooker bowl, combine onion, garlic, sweet potatoes, parsnips, apricots, coriander, cumin, and cinnamon. Top with lamb, any juices in bowl, and broth mixture; do not stir. Cover slow cooker and cook on Low for 8 hours.

4   After lamb has cooked, prepare couscous as label directs.

5   Skim and discard fat from cooking liquid. Reserve ¼ cup chopped olives; stir remaining olives into lamb mixture.

6   Spoon lamb mixture over couscous in bowls. Sprinkle with reserved chopped olives. Garnish with cilantro.

EACH SERVING: ABOUT 475 CALORIES | 44G PROTEIN | 50G CARBOHYDRATE | 11G TOTAL FAT (3G SATURATED) | 116MG CHOLESTEROL | 600MG SODIUM

HEARTY CHICKEN AND VEGETABLE STEW

A creamy sauce coats juicy chunks of chicken and a colorful array of vegetables in a dish that's pure comfort food.

ACTIVE TIME: 45 MINUTES · TOTAL TIME: 1 HOUR 20 MINUTES
MAKES: 4 MAIN-DISH SERVINGS

2	LEEKS (4 OUNCES EACH)	1	BAY LEAF
1	FENNEL BULB (1 POUND)	¼	TEASPOON DRIED TARRAGON LEAVES
2	TABLESPOONS OLIVE OIL	½	CUP DRY WHITE WINE
2	TABLESPOONS BUTTER OR MARGARINE	1	CAN (14½ OUNCES) CHICKEN BROTH
1	POUND SKINLESS, BONELESS CHICKEN-BREAST HALVES, CUT INTO 1½-INCH PIECES	¼	CUP WATER
		¾	CUP HALF-AND-HALF OR LIGHT CREAM
8	OUNCES MUSHROOMS, THICKLY SLICED	3	TABLESPOONS ALL-PURPOSE FLOUR
3	CARROTS (8 OUNCES TOTAL), PEELED AND CUT INTO 1-INCH PIECES	1	CUP FROZEN PEAS, THAWED
		¾	TEASPOON SALT
12	OUNCES RED POTATOES, CUT INTO 1-INCH PIECES		

1 Cut off root ends from leeks and trim leaf ends; cut each leek lengthwise in half and separate leaves. Rinse well with cold running water to remove any sand. Cut leeks crosswise into ¾-inch pieces.

2 Cut root end and stalks from fennel bulb; discard. Cut the fennel bulb lengthwise into thin wedges.

3 In 5-quart Dutch oven or saucepot, heat 1 tablespoon oil over medium-high heat until hot. Add 1 tablespoon butter; melt. Add chicken and cook until chicken is golden and just loses its pink color throughout. With slotted spoon, transfer chicken to medium bowl.

4 To drippings in Dutch oven, add mushrooms and cook, stirring often, until golden (do not over-brown). Transfer to bowl with chicken.

5 To Dutch oven, add remaining 1 tablespoon oil; heat until hot. Add remaining 1 tablespoon butter; melt. Add carrots, leeks, fennel, potatoes, bay leaf, and tarragon. Cook vegetables 10 to 15 minutes, until fennel is translucent and leeks are wilted, stirring occasionally.

6   Add wine; cook 2 minutes, stirring. Add broth and water; heat to boiling over high heat. Reduce heat to low; cover and simmer 20 minutes or until vegetables are tender.

7   In cup, mix half-and-half and flour until smooth. Stir half-and-half mixture into vegetable mixture; heat to boiling over high heat. Reduce heat to medium; cook 1 minute to thicken slightly. Stir in chicken, mushrooms, peas, and salt; heat through. Discard bay leaf.

EACH SERVING: ABOUT 530 CALORIES | 37G PROTEIN | 53G CARBOHYDRATE | 20G TOTAL FAT (5G SATURATED) | 85MG CHOLESTEROL | 985MG SODIUM 🍲

CHICKEN WITH ROSEMARY DUMPLINGS

What could be more comforting than chicken and dumplings? This version uses chicken breasts rather than a whole chicken to speed up the cooking time. The tender dumplings are cooked in the same pot and make this stew a complete meal. See "Delightful Dumplings," opposite, for tips.

ACTIVE TIME: 15 MINUTES · TOTAL TIME: 1 HOUR
MAKES: 6 MAIN-DISH SERVINGS

- 2 TABLESPOONS VEGETABLE OIL
- 6 LARGE BONE-IN CHICKEN-BREAST HALVES (3¼ POUNDS), SKIN REMOVED
- 4 LARGE CARROTS, PEELED AND CUT INTO 1-INCH PIECES
- 2 LARGE STALKS CELERY, CUT INTO ¼-INCH PIECES
- 1 MEDIUM ONION, FINELY CHOPPED
- 1 CUP PLUS 2 TABLESPOONS ALL-PURPOSE FLOUR
- 2 TEASPOONS BAKING POWDER
- 1½ TEASPOONS CHOPPED FRESH ROSEMARY, OR ½ TEASPOON DRIED ROSEMARY, CRUMBLED

- 1 TEASPOON SALT
- 1 LARGE EGG
- 1½ CUPS MILK
- 2 CUPS WATER
- 1 CAN (14½ OUNCES) LOW-SODIUM CHICKEN BROTH
- ¼ TEASPOON GROUND BLACK PEPPER
- 1 PACKAGE (10 OUNCES) FROZEN PEAS

1   In 8-quart Dutch oven, heat 1 tablespoon oil over medium-high heat until very hot. Add 3 chicken-breast halves; cook until golden brown, about 5 minutes per side. With slotted spoon, transfer chicken pieces to bowl as they are browned. Repeat with remaining chicken.

2   Add remaining 1 tablespoon oil to drippings in pot. Add carrots, celery, and onion and cook, stirring frequently, until golden brown and tender, about 10 minutes.

3   Meanwhile, prepare dumplings: In a small bowl, combine 1 cup flour, baking powder, rosemary, and ½ teaspoon salt. In cup, with fork, beat eggs with ½ cup milk. Stir egg mixture into flour mixture until just blended.

4   Return chicken to pot; add water, broth, pepper, and remaining ½ teaspoon salt. Heat to boiling on high. Drop dumpling mixture by rounded tablespoons on top of chicken to make 12 dumplings. Reduce heat to medium; cover and simmer 15 minutes.

DELIGHTFUL DUMPLINGS

Savory dumplings are small or large mounds of dough that are typically scooped then dropped into a soup, stew, or other hot liquid and cooked until done. Some are stuffed with meat or cheese mixtures; others are flavored with aromatics, like the rosemary used in the dumpling recipe opposite.

It's not difficult to make melt-in-your-mouth dumplings. During cooking, just be sure that the pot stays covered and the cooking liquid never exceeds a simmer. (If you boil the dumplings, they may fall apart.) A slotted spoon comes in handy when transferring the dumplings from the pot to a serving bowl.

5   With slotted spoon, transfer dumplings, chicken, and vegetables to serving bowl; keep warm. In cup, blend remaining 2 tablespoons flour with remaining 1 cup milk until smooth; stir into broth mixture in pot. Heat to boiling on high; boil 1 minute to thicken slightly. Add peas and heat through. Pour sauce over chicken and dumplings.

EACH SERVING: ABOUT 435 CALORIES | 46G PROTEIN | 38G CARBOHYDRATE | 10G TOTAL FAT (3G SATURATED) | 137MG CHOLESTEROL | 951MG SODIUM ☺

BLACK BEAN AND CHICKEN TORTILLA SOUP

This satisfying chicken soup has three major players: black beans, golden-browned chicken thighs, and spicy Mexican-style seasonings.

ACTIVE TIME: 25 MINUTES · **TOTAL TIME:** 35 MINUTES
MAKES: 8 MAIN-DISH SERVINGS

1 TABLESPOON VEGETABLE OIL	4 CUPS REDUCED-SODIUM CHICKEN BROTH
1½ POUNDS BONELESS, SKINLESS CHICKEN THIGHS, CUT INTO ½-INCH-WIDE STRIPS	2 CUPS WATER
½ TEASPOON SALT	1 CUP FROZEN CORN KERNELS
1 LARGE ONION (12 OUNCES), CHOPPED	2 CANS (16 OUNCES EACH) BLACK BEANS, RINSED AND DRAINED
2 POBLANO CHILES (3 OUNCES EACH), SEEDED AND CHOPPED	¼ CUP FRESH LIME JUICE
2 GARLIC CLOVES, CRUSHED WITH GARLIC PRESS	¼ CUP LOOSELY PACKED FRESH CILANTRO LEAVES, CHOPPED
1½ TEASPOONS GROUND CUMIN	2 CUPS COARSELY BROKEN TORTILLA CHIPS
1 TEASPOON GROUND CORIANDER	

1   In 6-quart saucepot, heat oil over medium-high heat until hot.

2   Sprinkle chicken with salt. Add chicken to saucepot in 2 batches and cook, stirring occasionally, until lightly browned, about 5 minutes per batch. With slotted spoon, transfer chicken to medium bowl.

3   After all chicken is browned, add onion, poblanos, and garlic to saucepot; cook over medium heat, stirring occasionally, until vegetables are lightly browned and tender, about 10 minutes. Stir in cumin and coriander; cook 1 minute. Add broth and water; cover and heat to boiling.

4   Return chicken, and any juices in bowl, to saucepot; stir in frozen corn and beans. Heat to boiling over medium-high heat; reduce heat to medium-low and simmer, uncovered, 10 minutes to blend flavors. Stir in lime juice and cilantro.

5   Ladle soup into bowls. Serve with tortilla chips to sprinkle on top.

EACH SERVING: ABOUT 240 CALORIES | 22G PROTEIN | 25G CARBOHYDRATE | 7G TOTAL FAT (1G SATURATED) | 71MG CHOLESTEROL | 625MG SODIUM ☺

CHICKEN AND SWEET-POTATO STEW

Coat chicken thighs with an exotic mix of cumin and cinnamon, then simmer with beta-carotene-rich sweet potatoes in a creamy peanut butter sauce. Delectable over brown rice.

ACTIVE TIME: 20 MINUTES · TOTAL TIME: 1 HOUR 5 MINUTES
MAKES: 4 MAIN-DISH SERVINGS

4 BONE-IN CHICKEN THIGHS (1½ POUNDS), SKIN REMOVED	3 TABLESPOONS NATURAL PEANUT BUTTER
1 TEASPOON GROUND CUMIN	½ TEASPOON SALT
¼ TEASPOON GROUND CINNAMON	¼ TEASPOON CRUSHED RED PEPPER
1 TABLESPOON OLIVE OIL	2 GARLIC CLOVES, PEELED
3 SWEET POTATOES (1½ POUNDS), PEELED AND CUT INTO ½-INCH CHUNKS	¼ CUP PACKED FRESH CILANTRO LEAVES PLUS 2 TABLESPOONS CHOPPED CILANTRO LEAVES
1 ONION, SLICED	
1 CAN (28 OUNCES) WHOLE TOMATOES IN JUICE	

1 Rub chicken thighs with cumin and cinnamon; set aside.

2 In nonstick 12-inch skillet, heat oil over medium heat. Add sweet potatoes and onion and cook until onion is tender, 12 to 15 minutes, stirring occasionally. Transfer sweet-potato mixture to plate.

3 Add seasoned chicken and cook 6 to 8 minutes or until chicken is lightly browned on both sides.

4 Meanwhile, drain tomatoes, reserving juice. Coarsely chop tomatoes and set aside. In blender at high speed or in food processor with knife blade attached, blend tomato juice, peanut butter, salt, crushed red pepper, garlic, and the ¼ cup cilantro leaves until smooth.

5 Add sweet-potato mixture, peanut-butter sauce, and chopped tomatoes to skillet with chicken; heat to boiling over medium-high heat. Reduce heat to low; cover and simmer 25 minutes or until juices run clear when chicken is pierced with tip of knife. To serve, sprinkle with chopped cilantro.

EACH SERVING: ABOUT 410 CALORIES | 26G PROTEIN | 50G CARBOHYDRATE | 12G TOTAL FAT (2G SATURATED) | 76MG CHOLESTEROL | 725MG SODIUM ☺ ▭

SPICY TURKEY CHILI

This luscious potful is made with leftover turkey, limas, and white beans—just right for a simple Sunday-evening supper. Sprinkle each serving with crushed baked corn chips if you want to add some crunch.

ACTIVE TIME: 20 MINUTES · TOTAL TIME: 40 MINUTES

MAKES: 6 CUPS OR 4 MAIN-DISH SERVINGS

1 TABLESPOON OLIVE OIL

1 ONION, CHOPPED

3 GARLIC CLOVES, MINCED

1½ TEASPOONS CHILI POWDER

1 TEASPOON GROUND CUMIN

1 TEASPOON GROUND CORIANDER

¼ TEASPOON SALT

¼ TEASPOON COARSELY GROUND BLACK PEPPER

1 CAN (15 TO 16 OUNCES) GREAT NORTHERN OR SMALL WHITE BEANS, RINSED AND DRAINED

1 CAN (14½ OUNCES) REDUCED-SODIUM CHICKEN BROTH

1 PACKAGE (10 OUNCES) FROZEN LIMA BEANS

1 CAN (4 TO 4½ OUNCES) CHOPPED MILD GREEN CHILES

2 CUPS BITE-SIZE PIECES LEFTOVER COOKED TURKEY OR CHICKEN MEAT (8 OUNCES)

1 CUP LOOSELY PACKED FRESH CILANTRO LEAVES, CHOPPED

2 TABLESPOONS FRESH LIME JUICE

LIME WEDGES (OPTIONAL)

1 In 5-quart Dutch oven, heat oil over medium heat until hot. Add onion and cook until tender, about 5 minutes, stirring often. Add garlic and cook 30 seconds. Stir in chili powder, cumin, coriander, salt, and pepper; cook 1 minute longer.

2 Meanwhile, in small bowl, mash half of Great Northern beans.

3 Add mashed beans and unmashed beans, broth, frozen lima beans, green chiles, and turkey meat to mixture in Dutch oven. Heat to boiling over medium-high heat. Reduce heat to low; cover and simmer 5 minutes to blend flavors. Remove Dutch oven from heat; stir in cilantro and lime juice. Serve with lime wedges if you like.

EACH SERVING: ABOUT 380 CALORIES | 33G PROTEIN | 45G CARBOHYDRATE | 8G TOTAL FAT (2G SATURATED) | 44MG CHOLESTEROL | 995MG SODIUM ☺ 🍴

MEDITERRANEAN SEAFOOD STEW

The fresh cod, shrimp, and mussels in this satisfying slow-cooker stew are added in the final forty minutes to keep their scrumptious flavor.

ACTIVE TIME: 20 MINUTES · **SLOW-COOK TIME:** 3 HOURS 30 MINUTES ON HIGH
MAKES: 6 MAIN-DISH SERVINGS

---

2 LARGE LEEKS, WHITE AND PALE GREEN PARTS ONLY	8 SPRIGS FRESH FLAT-LEAF PARSLEY, STEMS AND LEAVES SEPARATED
1½ POUNDS FENNEL (2 LARGE BULBS), TRIMMED AND FINELY CHOPPED	1 POUND MUSSELS, BEARDS REMOVED, SCRUBBED
2¼ POUNDS TOMATOES, CHOPPED	1 POUND SHRIMP (16 TO 20 COUNT), SHELLED AND DEVEINED
2 GARLIC CLOVES, CHOPPED	12 OUNCES SKINLESS COD FILLET, CUT INTO 4-INCH PIECES
1 TEASPOON SALT	
½ TEASPOON FRESHLY GROUND BLACK PEPPER	2 TEASPOONS EXTRA-VIRGIN OLIVE OIL
4 SPRIGS FRESH THYME	4 CRUSTY DINNER ROLLS

1   Cut off root ends from leeks and trim leaf ends. Cut each leek lengthwise in half, then into ¼-inch-thick slices. Place in large bowl of cold water. With hands, swish leeks to remove grit. Repeat process, changing water several times. Drain.

2   Transfer leeks to 6-quart slow-cooker bowl along with fennel, tomatoes, garlic, salt, and pepper. With kitchen twine, tie thyme and parsley stems together, reserving the parsley leaves. Bury in vegetable mixture.

3   Cover with lid and cook on High 3 hours. Stir in mussels and shrimp, and lay fish on top. Immediately cover and cook 30 to 40 minutes longer, or until mussels open and shrimp and fish turn opaque throughout.

4   Divide mussels among serving dishes. Discard herb bundle. Divide stew among serving dishes. Drizzle oil over stew. Chop reserved parsley leaves and sprinkle over stew. Serve with rolls.

EACH SERVING: 375 CALORIES | 32G PROTEIN | 46G CARBOHYDRATE | 7G TOTAL FAT (1G SATURATED) | 112MG CHOLESTEROL | 1,250MG SODIUM 🍲 🍲

SHRIMP AND SAUSAGE GUMBO

Fast and filling, this okra-thickened Creole classic delivers a hit of New Orleans spice. For photo, see page 14.

ACTIVE TIME: 30 MINUTES · TOTAL TIME: 1 HOUR

MAKES: 10 MAIN-DISH SERVINGS

- 1 POUND HOT ITALIAN SAUSAGE LINKS, PRICKED SEVERAL TIMES WITH FORK
- 3 TABLESPOONS VEGETABLE OIL
- ¼ CUP ALL-PURPOSE FLOUR
- 1 MEDIUM GREEN PEPPER, CHOPPED
- 1 MEDIUM ONION, CHOPPED
- 2 MEDIUM CELERY STALKS, CHOPPED
- 2 GARLIC CLOVES, FINELY CHOPPED
- 1 CAN (14 TO 14½ OUNCES) CHICKEN BROTH (1¾ CUPS)
- 1 CAN (14½ OUNCES) STEWED TOMATOES
- 1 CUP WATER
- 1 PACKAGE (10 OUNCES) FROZEN SLICED OKRA, THAWED
- 1 BAY LEAF
- ¼ TEASPOON DRIED OREGANO
- ¼ TEASPOON DRIED THYME
- ½ TEASPOON SALT
- 1½ CUPS REGULAR LONG-GRAIN WHITE RICE
- 1½ POUNDS SHELLED AND DEVEINED SHRIMP, WITH TAIL PART OF SHELL LEFT ON IF YOU LIKE

1 Heat 6-quart Dutch oven on medium-high. Add sausage and cook 8 minutes or until well browned, turning frequently. Transfer sausages to plate to cool slightly, then cut into ½-inch-thick diagonal slices.

2 While sausages cool, discard all but 1 tablespoon drippings from Dutch oven. Add oil to Dutch oven and heat on medium. (If your sausages are very lean and you do not get 1 tablespoon drippings, add enough additional oil to drippings to equal ¼ cup fat total.) Gradually stir flour into drippings until blended, and cook 4 to 5 minutes or until flour mixture (roux) is deep brown, stirring constantly. Add green pepper, onion, celery, and garlic, and cook 5 minutes or until all vegetables are tender, stirring occasionally.

3 Return sausages to Dutch oven; stir in broth, tomatoes, water, okra, bay leaf, oregano, thyme, and ¼ teaspoon salt.

4 Meanwhile, prepare rice as label directs. In medium bowl, toss shrimp with remaining ¼ teaspoon salt. Add shrimp to Dutch oven; cook 2 to 3 minutes or until opaque throughout. Discard bay leaf.

5 Serve gumbo in large bowls. Top each serving with a scoop of rice.

EACH SERVING: ABOUT 400 CALORIES | 25G PROTEIN | 33G CARBOHYDRATE | 17G TOTAL FAT (5G SATURATED) | 135MG CHOLESTEROL | 680MG SODIUM ☺ 🍲

CURRIED VEGETABLE STEW

This vegetarian meal is as easy as it is delicious. For extra crunch, sprinkle with toasted slivered almonds just before serving.

ACTIVE TIME: 15 MINUTES · TOTAL TIME: 40 MINUTES

MAKES: 4 MAIN-DISH SERVINGS

2 TEASPOONS OLIVE OIL	1½ TEASPOONS CURRY POWDER (SEE TIP)
1 LARGE SWEET POTATO (12 OUNCES), PEELED AND CUT INTO ½-INCH PIECES	1 TEASPOON GROUND CUMIN
1 MEDIUM ONION, CUT INTO ½-INCH PIECES	1 CAN (15 TO 19 OUNCES) GARBANZO BEANS, RINSED AND DRAINED
1 MEDIUM ZUCCHINI (8 OUNCES), CUT INTO 1-INCH PIECES	1 CAN (14½ OUNCES) DICED TOMATOES
1 SMALL GREEN PEPPER, CUT INTO ¼-INCH PIECES	¾ CUP VEGETABLE BROTH
	½ TEASPOON SALT

1 In deep nonstick 12-inch skillet, heat oil over medium. Add sweet potato, onion, zucchini, and green pepper; cook, stirring, until vegetables are tender, 10 to 12 minutes. Add curry powder and cumin; cook 1 minute.

2 Add garbanzo beans, tomatoes with their juice, broth, and salt; heat to boiling over medium-high heat. Reduce heat to medium-low; cover skillet and simmer until vegetables are very tender but still hold their shape, about 10 minutes longer.

TIP Curry powders can range from mild to hot—use whatever type you like best.

EACH SERVING: ABOUT 225 CALORIES | 8G PROTEIN | 39G CARBOHYDRATE | 5G TOTAL FAT (0G SATURATED) | 0MG CHOLESTEROL | 790MG SODIUM ☺ ▥

GINGER-SPICED CARROT SOUP

With one-and-a-half pounds of pureed carrots and two cups of peas, this creamy-smooth vegetable soup is supercharged with vitamin A, a vision-enhancing nutrient. Subbing ginger-steeped green tea for stock slashes the sodium, and may help protect against memory loss.

ACTIVE TIME: 25 MINUTES · TOTAL TIME: 55 MINUTES

MAKES: 4 MAIN-DISH SERVINGS

4   GREEN ONIONS

1   (1-INCH) PIECE FRESH GINGER

5   CUPS WATER

3   BAGS GREEN TEA

1   TABLESPOON OLIVE OIL

1   MEDIUM ONION, FINELY CHOPPED

1½ POUNDS CARROTS, PEELED AND CUT INTO ¾-INCH-THICK PIECES

1   MEDIUM ALL-PURPOSE POTATO, PEELED AND CHOPPED

½   TEASPOON SALT

¼   TEASPOON GROUND BLACK PEPPER

2   CUPS FROZEN PEAS

1   From green onions, cut off white and pale green parts and place in 5-quart saucepot. Thinly slice dark green onion parts; set aside. From ginger, cut 4 thin slices; set aside. Peel remaining piece of ginger and grate enough to make 1 teaspoon; set aside.

2   To saucepot, add sliced ginger and water. Heat to boiling over high heat. Add tea bags. Cover, remove from heat, and let stand 10 minutes.

3   While tea steeps, in 12-inch skillet, heat oil over medium-high heat. Add onion, carrots, potato, and ¼ teaspoon each salt and pepper. Cook, stirring, 6 minutes or until golden. Add grated ginger; cook 1 minute, stirring.

4   With slotted spoon, remove ginger, tea bags, and green onion pieces from pot and discard after squeezing excess liquid back into pot. Heat ginger tea to boiling over high heat; stir in carrot mixture. Reduce heat to maintain simmer. Cook 10 minutes or until vegetables are tender, stirring.

5   Transfer half of soup to blender; keep remaining soup simmering. Carefully puree until smooth, then return to pot. Stir in peas and remaining ¼ teaspoon salt. Cook 3 minutes or until peas are bright green and hot. Divide among soup bowls; garnish with sliced green onions.

EACH SERVING: 205 CALORIES | 7G PROTEIN | 37G CARBOHYDRATE | 4G TOTAL FAT (1G SATURATED) | 0MG CHOLESTEROL | 410MG SODIUM ☺ ♥

CREAMY ITALIAN WHITE-BEAN SOUP

Canned beans make this Tuscan classic a snap. But, if you have the time, substitute dried beans—they'll make this soup even more delicious. For this recipe, prepare two cups dried beans; they'll double in volume during soaking and cooking. See "Better Beans," opposite, for instructions.

ACTIVE TIME: 15 MINUTES · TOTAL TIME: 55 MINUTES
MAKES: 6 CUPS OR 4 MAIN-DISH SERVINGS

1   TABLESPOON VEGETABLE OIL
1   ONION, FINELY CHOPPED
1   CELERY STALK, FINELY CHOPPED
1   GARLIC CLOVE, MINCED
2   CANS (15½ TO 19 OUNCES EACH): WHITE KIDNEY BEANS (CANNELLINI), RINSED AND DRAINED
1   CAN (13¾ TO 14½ OUNCES) CHICKEN BROTH (1¾ CUPS)
¼   TEASPOON COARSELY GROUND BLACK PEPPER
⅛   TEASPOON DRIED THYME LEAVES
2   CUPS WATER
1   BUNCH (10 TO 12 OUNCES) SPINACH
1   TABLESPOON FRESH LEMON JUICE
FRESHLY GRATED PARMESAN CHEESE (OPTIONAL)

1   In 3-quart saucepan, heat oil over medium heat until hot. Add onion and celery and cook 5 to 8 minutes, until tender, stirring occasionally. Add garlic; cook 30 seconds, stirring. Add beans, chicken broth, pepper, thyme, and water; heat to boiling over high heat. Reduce heat to low; simmer, uncovered, 15 minutes.

2   Meanwhile, discard tough stems from spinach; thinly slice leaves.

3   With slotted spoon, remove 2 cups bean-and-vegetable mixture from soup; set aside. In blender at low speed, with center part of cover removed to allow steam to escape, blend remaining soup in small batches until smooth. Pour pureed soup into large bowl after each batch.

4   Return soup to saucepan; stir in reserved beans and vegetables. Heat to boiling over high heat, stirring occasionally. Stir in spinach and cook 1 minute or until wilted. Stir in lemon juice and remove from heat. Serve with Parmesan if you like.

EACH SERVING: ABOUT 295 CALORIES | 8G PROTEIN | 46G CARBOHYDRATE | 5G TOTAL FAT (1G SATURATED) | 0MG CHOLESTEROL | 945MG SODIUM ☺ ▤

BETTER BEANS

Dried beans that have been soaked and cooked are tastier and firmer than canned beans—plus they contain less sodium. To prepare them from scratch, sort through the dried beans to remove any tiny stones or debris, then rinse well under cold running water; drain.

To rehydrate the beans, transfer them to a pot and add enough water to cover the beans by two inches; allow the beans to soak until they have swelled to about double their size, four hours or overnight. Or, if you're short on time, combine the beans and water in a pot, heat to boiling, and cook for about three minutes. Remove from heat, cover tightly, and set aside for one hour to rehydrate; drain and rinse the beans.

The cook time for dried beans varies enormously: Use the time specified on the package as a guide, tasting to check for doneness often as the end of cook time approaches. To cook the beans, add fresh water to cover and a little salt to the pot, then cook according to package directions. Adding salt to the beans at the beginning toughens the skin and increases the cooking time, but beans taste better when seasoned early, so we use a minimal amount of salt at the beginning, then add the remainder near the end of the cook time. When done, drain the beans, reserving the cooking water to add flavor to your dish, if you like.

One cup dried beans averages two cups cooked beans, although the volume varies slightly among different bean varieties. Large beans, like limas, yield about two-and-one-half cups; small beans, such as black beans, yield just under two cups.

THREE-BEAN VEGETABLE CHILI

Hearty and colorful, this chili gets a wallop of flavor from a chipotle pepper (see Tip, opposite). If you can't find canned chipotles in adobo or chipotle chili powder, add one or two additional fresh jalapeños, including the seeds for more heat. You can vary the beans according to what you have on hand, as long as you have three cups dried in all. For soaking and draining instructions, see "Better Beans" on page 39. Serve the chili with tortilla chips.

ACTIVE TIME: 25 MINUTES · TOTAL TIME: 1 HOUR 45 MINUTES PLUS SOAKING BEANS
MAKES: 10 CUPS OR 6 MAIN-DISH SERVINGS

1 CUP DRY WHITE KIDNEY BEANS (CANNELLINI), SOAKED AND DRAINED	½ TEASPOON GROUND CORIANDER
1 CUP DRY RED KIDNEY BEANS, SOAKED AND DRAINED	⅛ TEASPOON GROUND CINNAMON
1 CUP DRY BLACK BEANS, SOAKED AND DRAINED	⅛ TEASPOON CAYENNE (GROUND RED) PEPPER
1 TABLESPOON OLIVE OR VEGETABLE OIL	1 CAN (28 OUNCES) TOMATOES IN PUREE
2 ONIONS, CHOPPED	1 CHIPOTLE CHILE IN ADOBO, FINELY CHOPPED, OR 1 TEASPOON GROUND CHIPOTLE CHILE (SEE TIP)
3 CARROTS, PEELED AND CHOPPED	2 TEASPOONS SALT
1 STALK CELERY, CHOPPED	¼ TEASPOON DRIED OREGANO
1 RED PEPPER, CHOPPED	2 CUPS WATER
3 GARLIC CLOVES, FINELY CHOPPED	1 PACKAGE (10 OUNCES) FROZEN WHOLE-KERNEL CORN, THAWED
1 JALAPEÑO CHILE, FINELY CHOPPED	½ CUP CHOPPED FRESH CILANTRO
2 TEASPOONS GROUND CUMIN	

1 In nonreactive 5-quart Dutch oven, combine all beans and enough *water* to cover by 2 inches; heat to boiling over high heat. Reduce heat; cover and simmer until beans are tender, about 1 hour. Drain beans and return to pan.

2 Meanwhile, in nonstick 10-inch skillet, heat oil over medium heat. Add onions, carrots, celery, and red pepper. Cook, stirring frequently, until carrots are tender, about 10 minutes. Stir in garlic, jalapeño, cumin, coriander, cinnamon, and cayenne; cook 30 seconds. Stir in tomatoes with their puree, chipotle chile, salt, and oregano, breaking up tomatoes with side of spoon. Heat to boiling; reduce heat and simmer 10 minutes, stirring several times.

3 Add tomato mixture and water to beans in Dutch oven; heat to boiling over medium-high heat. Reduce heat; cover and simmer, stirring occasionally, 15 minutes. Stir in corn and cook 5 minutes longer. Remove from heat and stir in ¼ cup cilantro. Spoon chili into bowls and sprinkle with remaining ¼ cup cilantro.

TIP Chipotles *en adobo* are dried, smoked red jalapeño peppers canned in a thick chile puree called *adobo*. They are available in the international section of many grocery stores or in Latin American markets. Chipotles may also be purchased dried and ground.

EACH SERVING: ABOUT 460 CALORIES | 25G PROTEIN | 86G CARBOHYDRATE | 4G TOTAL FAT
(1G SATURATED) | 0MG CHOLESTEROL | 1,048MG SODIUM

STOVETOP SUPPERS

Get out your nonstick skillet and toss together one of our stir-fries: Cashew chicken, steak and vegetables, and spicy pork and peanut can all be ready in a flash. In the mood for comfort food? Our Smothered Pork Chops offer down-home goodness in a jiffy. Or, if you're craving takeout, make our Fast Fried Rice: It'll be out of the skillet and on your table in just 15 minutes—speedier than the delivery man could get to your front door.

KEY TO ICONS

☺ 30 minutes or less   ♥ Heart healthy   ☺ Low calorie   ▭ Make ahead   🍲 Slow cooker

Chicken Dill Sauté (page 45)

CASHEW CHICKEN STIR-FRY

This stir-fry is a wonderfully quick and balanced meal: It delivers lots of protein from the chicken and cashews along with a nice variety of healthy greens.

ACTIVE TIME: 25 MINUTES · **TOTAL TIME:** 45 MINUTES
MAKES: 4 MAIN-DISH SERVINGS

- 1 CUP JASMINE RICE OR LONG-GRAIN WHITE RICE
- ½ CUP CANNED CHICKEN BROTH
- ¼ CUP DRY SHERRY
- 2 TABLESPOONS SOY SAUCE
- 1 TABLESPOON CORNSTARCH
- 1 TABLESPOON GRATED, PEELED FRESH GINGER
- 1 TEASPOON BROWN SUGAR
- ¼ TEASPOON SALT
- 2 TABLESPOONS VEGETABLE OIL
- 8 OUNCES ASPARAGUS, TRIMMED AND CUT INTO 2-INCH PIECES
- 4 OUNCES SNOW PEAS, STRINGS REMOVED AND EACH CUT IN HALF
- 2 LARGE CARROTS, PEELED AND CUT INTO 2" BY ⅛" MATCHSTICK-THIN STRIPS
- 1 BUNCH GREEN ONIONS, CUT INTO 2-INCH PIECES
- ½ CUP UNSALTED CASHEWS
- 1 POUND SKINLESS, BONELESS CHICKEN-BREAST HALVES, THINLY SLICED CROSSWISE

1 Prepare rice as label directs.

2 Meanwhile, in small bowl, whisk broth, sherry, soy sauce, cornstarch, ginger, brown sugar, and salt; set aside.

3 In 12-inch skillet, heat 1 tablespoon oil over medium-high heat until hot. Add asparagus and snow peas and cook 4 minutes or until tender-crisp, stirring frequently. Transfer vegetables to large bowl. To same skillet, add carrots, green onions, and cashews; cook 3 minutes, stirring frequently. Transfer to bowl with asparagus.

4 In same skillet, heat remaining 1 tablespoon oil. Add half of chicken and cook 2 to 3 minutes or just until chicken loses its pink color throughout, stirring constantly. With slotted spoon, transfer chicken to bowl with vegetables. Repeat with remaining chicken.

5 Stir broth mixture and add to skillet; heat to boiling, stirring. Boil 1 minute. Return vegetables and chicken to skillet; heat through. Serve with rice.

EACH SERVING: ABOUT 525 CALORIES | 35G PROTEIN | 58G CARBOHYDRATE | 17G TOTAL FAT (3G SATURATED) | 66MG CHOLESTEROL | 870MG SODIUM

CHICKEN DILL SAUTÉ

To keep this lemony spring chicken dish lean and luscious, sear the meat in a little oil first, then add water. This keeps the meat and vegetables from sticking to the pan—and helps make a flavorful sauce. For photo, see page 42.

ACTIVE TIME: 30 MINUTES · **TOTAL TIME:** 40 MINUTES

MAKES: 4 MAIN-DISH SERVINGS

---

1 LEMON

1 POUND SKINLESS, BONELESS CHICKEN-BREAST HALVES, CUT INTO ½-INCH CHUNKS

3 TEASPOONS EXTRA-VIRGIN OLIVE OIL

1 SMALL ONION, THINLY SLICED

2 LARGE PEPPERS, ORANGE AND YELLOW, SLICED

½ CUP WATER

⅞ TEASPOON SALT

⅜ TEASPOON GROUND BLACK PEPPER

8 OUNCES SUGAR SNAP PEAS, STRINGS REMOVED, CUT IN HALF

⅓ CUP FRESH DILL, CHOPPED

1 From lemon, grate 1 teaspoon peel; set aside. Into pie plate, squeeze 1 tablespoon juice. Add chicken; turn to coat.

2 In 12-inch skillet, heat 1 teaspoon oil over medium-high heat. Add onion, peppers, 2 tablespoons water, and ¼ teaspoon each salt and pepper. Cook 3 minutes or until softened, stirring. Transfer to large plate.

3 In same skillet, heat 1 teaspoon oil over medium-high heat. Add peas, 2 tablespoons water, ⅛ teaspoon salt, and remaining ⅛ teaspoon pepper. Cook, stirring occasionally, 2 to 3 minutes or until beginning to brown. Add to bell pepper mixture.

4 In same skillet, heat remaining 1 teaspoon oil over medium-high heat. Add chicken; sprinkle with ¼ teaspoon salt. Cook 3 minutes or until golden, stirring once. Return vegetables to pan; add remaining ¼ cup water. Cook 1 minute or until saucy, stirring. Stir in dill, remaining ¼ teaspoon salt, and reserved lemon peel.

EACH SERVING: ABOUT 230 CALORIES | 27G PROTEIN | 14G CARBOHYDRATE | 7G TOTAL FAT (1G SATURATED) | 73MG CHOLESTEROL | 650MG SODIUM ☺

THAI CHICKEN WITH ASPARAGUS

A trio of Asian seasonings—ginger, chiles, and fish sauce—turns up the heat in this skillet dinner. If you prefer, use fresh green beans instead of the asparagus. Serve over rice, if you like.

ACTIVE TIME: 25 MINUTES · **TOTAL TIME:** 55 MINUTES
MAKES: 4 MAIN-DISH SERVINGS

1 TEASPOON SALT	3 TEASPOONS VEGETABLE OIL
1 POUND THIN ASPARAGUS, TRIMMED AND CUT DIAGONALLY INTO 3-INCH PIECES	1 JUMBO ONION (1 POUND), THINLY SLICED
1 TABLESPOON SUGAR	1 PIECE FRESH GINGER (2" BY 1"), PEELED AND CUT INTO MATCHSTICK-THIN STRIPS
3 TABLESPOONS ASIAN FISH SAUCE (SEE TIP)	
2 TABLESPOONS FRESH LIME JUICE	2 JALAPEÑO CHILES, SEEDED AND CUT INTO MATCHSTICK-THIN STRIPS
1 TABLESPOON PLUS 1 TEASPOON SOY SAUCE	2 CUPS PACKED FRESH BASIL LEAVES
1¼ POUNDS SKINLESS, BONELESS CHICKEN-BREAST HALVES, THINLY SLICED	1 CUP PACKED FRESH CILANTRO LEAVES

1 In 10-inch skillet, heat 1 *inch water* and salt to boiling over high heat. Add asparagus; heat to boiling. Reduce heat to low; simmer, uncovered, 3 to 5 minutes, until asparagus is just tender-crisp. Drain asparagus; set aside.

2 In medium bowl, mix sugar, fish sauce, lime juice, and soy sauce. Stir in chicken until evenly coated. (Coat chicken just before cooking because the lime juice will change its texture.)

3 In nonstick 12-inch skillet, heat 2 teaspoons oil over medium heat until hot. Add chicken and cook 6 minutes or just until it loses its pink color throughout, stirring occasionally. With tongs or slotted spoon, transfer chicken to a clean bowl, leaving any cooking liquid in skillet.

4 Add onion, ginger, and jalapeños to skillet and cook until onion is tender, about 8 minutes. Transfer onion mixture to bowl with the cooked chicken.

5 In same skillet, heat remaining 1 teaspoon oil over medium heat until hot. Add the asparagus to the skillet and cook until it begins to brown, about 5 minutes, stirring occasionally. Return onion mixture and chicken to skillet; heat through.

6 Toss basil and cilantro with chicken mixture just before serving.

TIP An integral flavoring in Southeast Asian cooking, fish sauce is made from fermented fish. It is available in the international section of many supermarkets or in Asian groceries, where it may be labeled *nam pla* (Thai) or *nuoc nam* (Vietnamese). Stored at cool room temperature in a dark place, Asian fish sauce will keep for about one year.

EACH SERVING: ABOUT 290 CALORIES | 38G PROTEIN | 21G CARBOHYDRATE | 6G TOTAL FAT (1G SATURATED) | 82MG CHOLESTEROL | 1,555MG SODIUM ☺

SKILLET ARROZ CON POLLO

This dish, popular in Spain and Mexico, literally means "rice with chicken." We've used chicken-breast tenders instead of bone-in pieces to shorten the cooking time.

ACTIVE TIME: 15 MINUTES · TOTAL TIME: 55 MINUTES

MAKES: 4 MAIN-DISH SERVINGS

- 1 TABLESPOON OLIVE OIL
- 1 ONION, FINELY CHOPPED
- 1 RED PEPPER, CUT INTO 1½-INCH PIECES
- 1 CUP LONG-GRAIN WHITE RICE
- 1 GARLIC CLOVE, MINCED
- ⅛ TEASPOON CAYENNE (GROUND RED) PEPPER
- 1 STRIP (3" BY ½") LEMON PEEL
- ¼ TEASPOON SALT
- 1 CAN (14½ OUNCES) CHICKEN BROTH

- ¼ CUP DRY SHERRY OR WATER
- 1 POUND CHICKEN-BREAST TENDERS, CUT INTO 2-INCH PIECES
- 1 CUP FROZEN PEAS
- ¼ CUP DRAINED SALAD OLIVES (CHOPPED PIMIENTO-STUFFED OLIVES)
- ½ CUP LOOSELY PACKED FRESH CILANTRO LEAVES OR PARSLEY LEAVES, CHOPPED

LEMON WEDGES FOR GARNISH

1 In 12-inch skillet, heat oil over medium heat until hot. Add onion and red pepper and cook until tender, about 12 minutes, stirring occasionally. Stir in rice, garlic, and cayenne; cook 2 minutes. Stir in lemon peel, salt, broth, and sherry; heat to boiling over medium-high heat. Reduce heat to low; cover and simmer 13 minutes.

2 Stir in chicken tenders; cover and simmer 13 minutes longer or until juices run clear when chicken is pierced with tip of knife and rice is tender, stirring once halfway through cooking time. Stir in frozen peas; cover and heat through. Remove skillet from heat; let stand 5 minutes.

3 To serve, stir in olives and sprinkle with cilantro. Pass lemon wedges to squeeze over each serving.

EACH SERVING: ABOUT 410 CALORIES | 34G PROTEIN | 49G CARBOHYDRATE | 7G TOTAL FAT (2G SATURATED) | 66MG CHOLESTEROL | 925MG SODIUM ☺

CHICKEN WITH SMOKED MOZZARELLA AND SQUASH

In this inventive dish, strands of spaghetti squash are tossed with chopped fresh tomato and smoked mozzarella to create a pasta-like base for the chicken. To speed up the cook time, we microwaved the squash.

TOTAL TIME: 25 MINUTES

MAKES: 4 MAIN-DISH SERVINGS

1 MEDIUM SPAGHETTI SQUASH (2½ POUNDS)	¼ TEASPOON COARSELY GROUND BLACK PEPPER
1 TABLESPOON OLIVE OIL	2 MEDIUM TOMATOES, CHOPPED
1 LARGE ONION (10 TO 12 OUNCES), THINLY SLICED	2 OUNCES SMOKED MOZZARELLA OR SMOKED GOUDA CHEESE
12 OUNCES BONELESS, SKINLESS CHICKEN-BREAST HALVES, THINLY SLICED CROSSWISE	¼ CUP LOOSELY PACKED FRESH BASIL LEAVES, THINLY SLICED
½ TEASPOON SALT	

1   With tip of sharp knife, pierce squash in about 10 places. Microwave on High 6 to 7 minutes. Turn squash over and pierce in another 10 places; microwave 6 to 7 minutes longer or until squash is soft to the touch.

2   Meanwhile, in nonstick 12-inch skillet, heat oil over medium heat. Add onion and cook until tender and golden, about 8 minutes, stirring occasionally. Add chicken, ¼ teaspoon salt, and ⅛ teaspoon pepper and cook until chicken loses its pink color throughout, about 8 minutes, stirring occasionally.

3   When squash is done, cut lengthwise in half; discard seeds. With fork, gently scrape squash lengthwise and lift out pulp in strands as it becomes free; place in large bowl. Discard squash skin.

4   Mix tomatoes, smoked mozzarella, and remaining ¼ teaspoon salt and ⅛ teaspoon pepper with hot squash. Spoon squash mixture into 4 serving bowls; top with onion and chicken mixture. Sprinkle with basil.

EACH SERVING: ABOUT 260 CALORIES | 25G PROTEIN | 20G CARBOHYDRATE | 9G TOTAL FAT (3G SATURATED) | 62MG CHOLESTEROL | 585MG SODIUM

STIR-FRIED STEAK AND VEGETABLES

This healthy-in-a-hurry recipe contains whole grains (brown rice), protein-rich beef (top round steak), and a rainbow of veggies.

ACTIVE TIME: 15 MINUTES · TOTAL TIME: 25 MINUTES

MAKES: 4 MAIN-DISH SERVINGS

- 1 BEEF TOP ROUND STEAK (1 POUND)
- ⅓ CUP REDUCED-SODIUM SOY SAUCE
- 2 GARLIC CLOVES, CRUSHED WITH GARLIC PRESS
- 1 ONION
- 1 RED PEPPER
- 2 TEASPOONS VEGETABLE OIL
- 8 OUNCES SLICED CREMINI MUSHROOMS
- 2 CUPS BROCCOLI FLORETS

- 2 CARROTS, PEELED AND THINLY SLICED
- 3 OUNCES SNOW PEAS, TRIMMED AND CUT INTO THIRDS
- 2 TABLESPOONS GRATED, PEELED FRESH GINGER
- ¾ CUP WATER
- 1 PACKAGE (8½ OUNCES) PRECOOKED BROWN RICE, HEATED AS LABEL DIRECTS

---

1   With knife held in slanting position, almost parallel to cutting surface, cut round steak crosswise into ⅛-inch-thick slices. In medium bowl, toss steak slices with 1 tablespoon soy sauce and 1 crushed garlic clove. Let stand 5 minutes.

2   Meanwhile, cut onion in half, then thinly slice crosswise. Cut red pepper into ¼-inch-thick slices. Set vegetables aside.

3   In deep nonstick 12-inch skillet, heat 1 teaspoon oil over medium heat until very hot but not smoking. Add half of beef and stir-fry 30 to 45 seconds or just until beef is no longer pink. Transfer beef to plate. Repeat with remaining beef, without adding additional oil.

4   In same skillet, heat remaining 1 teaspoon oil until hot. Add mushrooms and onion; cover and cook 3 to 4 minutes or until mushrooms are browned, stirring occasionally.

5   Add broccoli, carrots, snow peas, red pepper, ginger, water, and remaining soy sauce and crushed garlic clove to skillet. Stir-fry until vegetables are tender-crisp, 5 to 6 minutes. Remove skillet from heat; stir in beef with its juices. Serve over rice.

EACH SERVING: ABOUT 380 CALORIES | 34G PROTEIN | 34G CARBOHYDRATE | 12G TOTAL FAT (4G SATURATED) | 68MG CHOLESTEROL | 790MG SODIUM ☺ ☺

STIR-FRIED BEEF WITH ARUGULA

For a speedy weeknight meal, there's nothing like a stir-fry. To round out the menu, serve this with chilled red grapes for dessert.

ACTIVE TIME: 10 MINUTES · **TOTAL TIME:** 20 MINUTES
MAKES: 4 MAIN-DISH SERVINGS

4	TEASPOONS VEGETABLE OIL	3	TABLESPOONS SOY SAUCE
1	BUNCH GREEN ONIONS, CUT INTO 1½-INCH PIECES	3	TABLESPOONS BALSAMIC VINEGAR
		2	TABLESPOONS BROWN SUGAR
8	OUNCES SLICED MUSHROOMS	2	BUNCHES ARUGULA, OR 2 PACKAGES (8 OUNCES EACH) PREWASHED SPINACH
1	POUND SLICED BEEF FOR STIR-FRY (SEE TIP)		

1 In nonstick 12-inch skillet, heat 2 teaspoons oil over medium heat. Add green onions and mushrooms and cook until tender and brown, 6 to 8 minutes, stirring often. Transfer to bowl.

2 In same skillet, heat 1 teaspoon oil. Add half the beef and cook, stirring constantly, until beef just loses its pink color. Transfer to bowl with vegetables. Cook remaining beef as above, adding remaining 1 teaspoon oil.

3 In cup, mix soy sauce, vinegar, and brown sugar. Return beef mixture to skillet; stir in soy-sauce mixture. Cook 1 minute to heat through, stirring. Remove from heat; stir in half the arugula.

4 Spoon the beef mixture over remaining arugula on platter.

TIP If you can't find precut beef, thinly slice a 1-pound piece of top round steak.

EACH SERVING: ABOUT 260 CALORIES | 29G PROTEIN | 18G CARBOHYDRATE | 15G TOTAL FAT (5G SATURATED) | 48MG CHOLESTEROL | 875MG SODIUM 😊 ☺

SPICY BEEF WITH COUSCOUS

This curry is on the milder side, so it's great for the whole family. The addition of raisins to the couscous lends an unexpected sweetness.

TOTAL TIME: 45 MINUTES

MAKES: 4 MAIN-DISH SERVINGS

1	TABLESPOON VEGETABLE OIL	½	TEASPOON SALT
1	ONION, CHOPPED	1	SMALL YELLOW SUMMER SQUASH
2	GARLIC CLOVES, CRUSHED WITH GARLIC PRESS		(6 OUNCES), CUT INTO ½-INCH CHUNKS
		1	CUP CANNED CHICKEN BROTH
1	TEASPOON MINCED, PEELED FRESH GINGER	1	CUP FROZEN PEAS
		½	CUP LOOSELY PACKED FRESH CILANTRO LEAVES, CHOPPED
1	POUND LEAN (90%) GROUND BEEF		
1	TABLESPOON CURRY POWDER	1	CUP PLAIN COUSCOUS
1	TEASPOON GARAM MASALA SPICE MIX	⅓	CUP GOLDEN RAISINS

1 In 12-inch skillet, heat oil over medium-high heat. Add onion and cook 3 minutes or until golden. Stir in garlic and ginger; cook 1 minute.

2 Stir in ground beef and cook, breaking up meat with side of spoon, about 5 minutes or until meat is no longer pink. Stir in curry powder, garam masala, and salt; cook 30 seconds. Add squash and cook 2 minutes.

3 Add broth and frozen peas; cook until slightly thickened and flavors blend. Stir in cilantro.

4 Meanwhile, prepare couscous as label directs but add raisins with water.

5 Fluff couscous with fork and serve with beef mixture.

EACH SERVING: ABOUT 520 CALORIES | 34G PROTEIN | 57G CARBOHYDRATE | 16G TOTAL FAT (5G SATURATED) | 69MG CHOLESTEROL | 650MG SODIUM

SMOTHERED PORK CHOPS

Thanks to a no-guilt mushroom gravy and meaty center-cut chops, this skinny version of the Southern classic is more hearty than heavy.

ACTIVE TIME: 20 MINUTES · **TOTAL TIME:** 50 MINUTES
MAKES: 4 MAIN-DISH SERVINGS

3   TABLESPOONS PLUS 1 TEASPOON WHITE WHOLE-WHEAT FLOUR (SEE TIP) OR ALL-PURPOSE FLOUR

½   TEASPOON SALT

½   TEASPOON GROUND BLACK PEPPER

4   BONELESS, CENTER-CUT PORK CHOPS (EACH 5 OUNCES, ¾ INCH THICK)

1   TABLESPOON CANOLA OIL

2   LARGE ONIONS, THINLY SLICED

3   GARLIC CLOVES, CHOPPED

1   POUND CREMINI MUSHROOMS, SLICED

½   TEASPOON DRIED ROSEMARY

1   CUP REDUCED-SODIUM CHICKEN BROTH

1   BAG (12 OUNCES) MICROWAVE-IN-THE-BAG GREEN BEANS

1   Sprinkle 1 teaspoon flour and ¼ teaspoon each salt and pepper all over pork chops. In 12-inch skillet, heat oil over medium-high heat. Add pork and cook 7 minutes or until browned, turning over once. Transfer to plate.

2   To same skillet, add onions and garlic. Reduce heat to medium and cook 5 minutes or until browned and softened, stirring frequently. Add mushrooms and rosemary; cook 6 to 8 minutes or until mushrooms are tender, stirring occasionally. Add remaining 3 tablespoons flour; cook 3 minutes, stirring constantly.

3   Add broth in slow, steady stream, stirring constantly. Heat to simmering and return pork to pan in single layer; spoon vegetable mixture on top. Cover; reduce heat and simmer 8 minutes or until pork is barely pink in center. (An instant-read thermometer inserted horizontally into center of chop should register 145°F.) Stir in remaining ¼ teaspoon each salt and pepper.

4   While pork simmers, cook beans as label directs. Arrange beans on plates with pork and sauce.

TIP   White whole-wheat flour makes your gravy just a tad bit healthier without sacrificing the smoothness or luscious flavor. Available from Gold Medal among other brands, it is milled from an albino variety of whole wheat.

EACH SERVING: ABOUT 395 CALORIES | 34G PROTEIN | 30G CARBOHYDRATE | 18G TOTAL FAT (6G SATURATED) | 74MG CHOLESTEROL | 955MG SODIUM ☺

KIELBASA AND RED CABBAGE

This stick-to-your-ribs skillet dish is worth the trip to a Polish butcher for some homemade kielbasa.

ACTIVE TIME: 15 MINUTES · TOTAL TIME: 1 HOUR
MAKES: 4 MAIN-DISH SERVINGS

2 TABLESPOONS BUTTER
   OR MARGARINE

1 SMALL ONION, CHOPPED

1 SMALL HEAD RED CABBAGE
   (1½ POUNDS), THINLY SLICED

2 GOLDEN DELICIOUS APPLES (SEE TIP),
   PEELED, CORED, AND THINLY SLICED

½ CUP APPLE JUICE

3 TABLESPOONS RED WINE VINEGAR

1 TABLESPOON SUGAR

1 TEASPOON SALT

1 POUND KIELBASA (SMOKED POLISH
   SAUSAGE), CUT CROSSWISE INTO
   2-INCH PIECES

1 In nonstick 10-inch skillet, melt butter over medium heat. Add onion and cook, stirring, until tender. Add cabbage, apples, apple juice, vinegar, sugar, and salt; heat to boiling. Reduce heat to low; cover skillet and simmer for 15 minutes.

2 Add kielbasa to cabbage mixture; heat to boiling over high heat. Reduce heat; cover and simmer 15 minutes.

EACH SERVING: ABOUT 525 CALORIES | 18G PROTEIN | 32G CARBOHYDRATE | 37G TOTAL FAT (15G SATURATED) | 92MG CHOLESTEROL | 1,883MG SODIUM

SPICY PEANUT PORK

Asian spices and peanut butter turn pork chops into a sensational supper. Try this tasty combination over steamed rice or Asian noodles.

TOTAL TIME: 30 MINUTES

MAKES: 4 MAIN-DISH SERVINGS

4 BONELESS CENTER-CUT PORK CHOPS (EACH 5 OUNCES, ¾-INCH THICK), WELL-TRIMMED

¼ TEASPOON COARSELY GROUND BLACK PEPPER

½ TEASPOON SALT

4 GREEN ONIONS, CUT INTO 1-INCH DIAGONAL SLICES

8 OUNCES SNOW PEAS, STRINGS REMOVED

1 TABLESPOON MINCED, PEELED FRESH GINGER

3 GARLIC CLOVES, CRUSHED WITH GARLIC PRESS

¼ CUP CREAMY PEANUT BUTTER

1 TABLESPOON SUGAR

1 TABLESPOON SOY SAUCE

⅛ TEASPOON CAYENNE (GROUND RED) PEPPER

¾ CUP WATER

1 Pat pork chops dry with paper towels. Sprinkle pork chops with pepper and ¼ teaspoon salt.

2 Heat nonstick 12-inch skillet over medium heat until hot. Add pork chops and cook 5 minutes; turn pork over and cook 4 to 5 minutes longer, until lightly browned on the outside and still slightly pink on the inside. Transfer pork to platter; cover with foil to keep warm.

3 To same skillet, add green onions, snow peas, and remaining ¼ teaspoon salt and cook over medium heat 4 minutes, stirring frequently. Stir in ginger and garlic; cook 1 minute. Return pork to skillet.

4 Meanwhile, in small bowl, stir peanut butter, sugar, soy sauce, cayenne, and water until blended.

5 Pour peanut-butter mixture into same skillet; heat to boiling over medium heat. Reduce heat to low; simmer 1 minute.

EACH SERVING: ABOUT 350 CALORIES | 37G PROTEIN | 13G CARBOHYDRATE | 17G TOTAL FAT (5G SATURATED) | 76MG CHOLESTEROL | 685MG SODIUM

FAST FRIED RICE

The speed secrets to this dish are quick-cooking brown rice, precut frozen vegetables, and ready-to-use stir-fry sauce. If you have leftover cooked rice, use four cups.

TOTAL TIME: 15 MINUTES

MAKES: 4 MAIN-DISH SERVINGS

1½ CUPS QUICK-COOKING BROWN RICE

1 POUND FIRM TOFU, DRAINED AND CUT INTO 1-INCH CUBES

2 TABLESPOONS OLIVE OIL

1 PACKAGE (16 OUNCES) FROZEN VEGETABLES FOR STIR-FRY

2 LARGE EGGS, LIGHTLY BEATEN

⅓ CUP STIR-FRY SAUCE

¼ CUP WATER

1 Prepare rice as label directs.

2 Meanwhile, in medium bowl, place 3 layers paper towels. Place tofu on towels and top with 3 more layers paper towels. Gently press the tofu with your hand to extract the excess moisture.

3 In nonstick 12-inch skillet, heat 2 teaspoons oil over medium heat until hot. Add frozen vegetables; cover and cook 5 minutes, stirring occasionally. Transfer vegetables to bowl; keep warm.

4 In same skillet, heat remaining 4 teaspoons oil until hot. Add tofu and cook 5 minutes, gently stirring. Stir in rice and cook 4 minutes longer.

5 With spatula, push rice mixture around edge of skillet, leaving space in center. Add eggs to center of skillet; cook 2 minutes, stirring eggs until scrambled. Add stir-fry sauce, vegetables, and water; cook 1 minute, stirring.

EACH SERVING: ABOUT 360 CALORIES | 17G PROTEIN | 41G CARBOHYDRATE | 15G TOTAL FAT (2G SATURATED) | 106MG CHOLESTEROL | 760MG SODIUM ☑ ☺

SHRIMP RISOTTO WITH BABY PEAS

Be sure to buy shrimp in the shells for this dish. Making a quick stock with the shells gives this pretty risotto a more complex flavor.

ACTIVE TIME: 35 MINUTES · TOTAL TIME: 1 HOUR 30 MINUTES
MAKES: 4 MAIN-DISH SERVINGS

4	CUPS WATER	1	TABLESPOON OLIVE OIL
1	CAN (14½ OUNCES) CHICKEN OR VEGETABLE BROTH	1	SMALL ONION, FINELY CHOPPED
1	POUND MEDIUM SHRIMP, SHELLED AND DEVEINED, SHELLS RESERVED	2	CUPS ARBORIO RICE (ITALIAN SHORT-GRAIN RICE) OR MEDIUM-GRAIN RICE
1	TABLESPOON BUTTER OR MARGARINE	½	CUP DRY WHITE WINE
1½	TEASPOONS SALT	1	CUP FROZEN BABY PEAS
⅛	TEASPOON GROUND BLACK PEPPER	¼	CUP CHOPPED FRESH PARSLEY

1 In 3-quart saucepan, combine water, broth, and shrimp shells. Heat to boiling over high heat. Reduce heat; simmer 20 minutes. Strain broth through sieve into bowl and measure. If needed, add *water* to equal 5½ cups. Return broth to same clean saucepan; heat to boiling. Reduce heat to maintain simmer; cover.

2 In 4-quart saucepan, melt butter over medium-high heat. Add shrimp, ½ teaspoon salt, and pepper; cook, stirring, just until the shrimp are opaque throughout, about 2 minutes. Transfer to bowl.

3 In same saucepan, heat oil over medium heat. Add onion and cook until tender, about 5 minutes. Add rice and remaining 1 teaspoon salt; cook, stirring frequently, until rice grains are opaque. Add wine; cook until wine has been absorbed. Add about ½ cup simmering broth to rice; stir until liquid has been absorbed. Continue cooking, adding remaining broth ½ cup at a time and stirring after each addition, until all liquid has been absorbed and rice is tender but still firm, about 25 minutes. (Risotto should have a creamy consistency.) Stir in frozen peas and shrimp and heat through. Stir in parsley.

EACH SERVING: ABOUT 510 CALORIES | 28G PROTEIN | 76G CARBOHYDRATE | 10G TOTAL FAT (3G SATURATED) | 148MG CHOLESTEROL | 1,532MG SODIUM

CHILI SCALLOPS WITH BLACK-BEAN SALSA

A light dusting of spices makes tender sea scallops taste really special. The flavorful cilantro-scented salsa can also be served as a side dish with grilled beef or chicken.

ACTIVE TIME: 15 MINUTES · TOTAL TIME: 20 MINUTES
MAKES: 4 MAIN-DISH SERVINGS

1 CAN (15 TO 19 OUNCES) BLACK BEANS, RINSED AND DRAINED

1 CAN (15¼ TO 16 OUNCES) WHOLE-KERNEL CORN, DRAINED

¼ CUP FINELY CHOPPED RED ONION

¼ CUP LOOSELY PACKED FRESH CILANTRO LEAVES, CHOPPED

2 TABLESPOONS FRESH LIME JUICE

½ TEASPOON SALT

1 POUND SEA SCALLOPS

1 TABLESPOON CHILI POWDER

1 TEASPOON SUGAR

2 TEASPOONS VEGETABLE OIL

CILANTRO LEAVES AND HOT RED CHILES FOR GARNISH

LIME WEDGES (OPTIONAL)

1   In large bowl, mix black beans, corn, onion, chopped cilantro, lime juice, and ¼ teaspoon salt. Set black-bean salsa aside.

2   Rinse scallops with cold running water to remove sand from crevices; pat dry with paper towels. In medium bowl, mix chili powder, sugar, and remaining ¼ teaspoon salt; add scallops, tossing to coat.

3   In nonstick 12-inch skillet, heat oil over medium-high heat until very hot. Add scallops and cook 3 to 6 minutes, until scallops are lightly browned on the outside and turn opaque throughout, turning once.

4   Arrange black-bean salsa and scallops on 4 dinner plates and garnish with cilantro leaves and red chiles. Serve with lime wedges if you like.

EACH SERVING: ABOUT 290 CALORIES | 31G PROTEIN | 40G CARBOHYDRATE | 5G TOTAL FAT (1G SATURATED) | 38MG CHOLESTEROL | 1,005MG SODIUM 🗸 ☺

CURRIED SWEET POTATOES AND LENTILS

This hearty vegetarian entrée tastes even better with a dollop of plain yogurt and a squeeze of fresh lime juice.

ACTIVE TIME: 15 MINUTES · **TOTAL TIME:** 45 MINUTES PLUS STANDING
MAKES: 4 MAIN-DISH SERVINGS

1 TABLESPOON OLIVE OIL

1 MEDIUM ONION, CHOPPED

2 GARLIC CLOVES, MINCED

1 TABLESPOON CURRY POWDER

3 MEDIUM SWEET POTATOES (1½ POUNDS), PEELED AND CUT INTO 1-INCH CHUNKS

1 CUP LENTILS, RINSED AND PICKED OVER

½ CUP LONG-GRAIN WHITE RICE

½ TEASPOON SALT

1 CAN (14½ OUNCES) VEGETABLE BROTH OR CHICKEN BROTH

2½ CUPS WATER

¼ CUP LOOSELY PACKED FRESH CILANTRO LEAVES

1 In nonstick 12-inch skillet, heat oil over medium heat until hot. Add onion and cook 5 minutes, stirring often. Add garlic and curry powder and cook 1 minute longer, stirring constantly.

2 Stir in sweet potatoes, lentils, rice, salt, broth, and water; heat to boiling over medium-high heat. Reduce heat to low; cover and simmer 30 minutes or until lentils and rice are tender and almost all liquid is absorbed. Let stand 5 minutes. Sprinkle with cilantro to serve.

EACH SERVING: ABOUT 460 CALORIES | 16G PROTEIN | 87G CARBOHYDRATE | 5G TOTAL FAT (1G SATURATED) | 0MG CHOLESTEROL | 630MG SODIUM

BUTTERNUT-SQUASH RISOTTO WITH SAGE

This requires a lot of attention at the range, but it's worth it. If you can, use Arborio rice—it makes the dish extra creamy.

ACTIVE TIME: 20 MINUTES · **TOTAL TIME:** 1 HOUR 10 MINUTES
MAKES: 4 MAIN-DISH SERVINGS

1 LARGE BUTTERNUT SQUASH (2½ POUNDS), PEELED

1 CAN (13¾ TO 14½ OUNCES) CHICKEN OR VEGETABLE BROTH

1 TABLESPOON BUTTER OR MARGARINE

¼ TEASPOON COARSELY GROUND BLACK PEPPER

3 TABLESPOONS CHOPPED FRESH SAGE

1 TEASPOON SALT

2 TABLESPOONS OLIVE OIL

1 SMALL ONION, FINELY CHOPPED

2 CUPS ARBORIO RICE (ITALIAN SHORT-GRAIN RICE) OR MEDIUM-GRAIN RICE

⅓ CUP DRY WHITE WINE

½ CUP GRATED PARMESAN CHEESE

1 Cut enough squash into ½-inch chunks to equal 3 cups. Coarsely shred enough remaining squash to equal 2 cups; set aside.

2 In 2-quart saucepan, heat broth and 4 *cups water* to boiling over high heat. Reduce heat to low to maintain simmer; cover.

3 In 5-quart Dutch oven or saucepot, melt butter over medium heat. Add squash chunks, pepper, 2 tablespoons sage, and ¼ teaspoon salt. Cook, covered, stirring occasionally, 10 minutes or until squash is tender. Remove squash to small bowl.

4 To same Dutch oven, add oil, shredded squash, onion, and remaining ¾ teaspoon salt and cook, stirring often, until vegetables are tender. Add rice and cook, stirring frequently, 2 minutes. Add wine; cook until absorbed. Add about ½ cup simmering broth to rice, stirring until liquid is absorbed.

5 Continue cooking, adding remaining broth ½ cup at a time and stirring after each addition, until all liquid is absorbed and rice is tender but still firm, about 25 minutes. (Risotto should have a creamy consistency.) Stir in squash chunks, Parmesan, and remaining 1 tablespoon chopped sage and heat through.

EACH SERVING: ABOUT 700 CALORIES | 17G PROTEIN | 115G CARBOHYDRATE | 4G TOTAL FAT (4G SATURATED) | 15MG CHOLESTEROL | 1,105MG SODIUM

PASTAS & PIES

Pastas and savory pies are one-dish meals everyone can agree on. Choose from oodles of noodles like Penne with Three Cheeses and Porcini Mushrooms, Beef and Sausage Lasagna, and a Greek Pasta Bowl with Shrimp. For delicious twists on comfort food classics, try our Veggie Mac 'n' Cheese and Tuna-Melt Casserole—or serve up a piping hot potpie. Savory pies aren't just for dinner: Our Potato-Crusted Quiche and Tomato-Cheese Pie are perfect for a weekend brunch.

KEY TO ICONS

✓ 30 minutes or less   ♥ Heart healthy   ☺ Low calorie   🍲 Make ahead   🍲 Slow cooker

Veggie Mac 'n' Cheese (page 76)

PENNE WITH THREE CHEESES

You won't miss the meat here, as dried porcini mushrooms lend a meaty, slightly nutty flavor to this hearty vegetarian dish.

ACTIVE TIME: 30 MINUTES · **TOTAL TIME:** 1 HOUR

MAKES: 8 MAIN-DISH SERVINGS

---

1   PACKAGE (16 OUNCES) PENNE RIGATE OR ZITI PASTA

1   CUP WATER

1   OUNCE DRIED PORCINI MUSHROOMS (1 CUP)

2   TABLESPOONS BUTTER OR MARGARINE

1   ONION, FINELY CHOPPED

1   TEASPOON FRESH THYME LEAVES, CHOPPED

3   TABLESPOONS ALL-PURPOSE FLOUR

2½ CUPS REDUCED-FAT (2%) MILK

⅛   TEASPOON GROUND NUTMEG

1   TEASPOON SALT

¼   TEASPOON GROUND BLACK PEPPER

4   OUNCES FONTINA CHEESE, CUBED

1   CUP PART-SKIM RICOTTA CHEESE

1   CUP FRESHLY GRATED PARMESAN CHEESE

1   In large saucepot, cook pasta 2 minutes less than label directs. Drain and return to pot.

2   Meanwhile, preheat oven to 375°F. In microwave-safe 4-cup liquid measuring cup, heat water in microwave oven on High 1½ to 2 minutes or until boiling. Stir in porcini mushrooms; let stand 15 minutes. With slotted spoon, remove porcini; rinse to remove any grit. Finely chop and set aside. Strain soaking liquid through sieve lined with paper towel and set aside.

3   In 4-quart saucepan, melt butter over medium heat. Add onion and cook 8 to 9 minutes or until tender and lightly browned, stirring occasionally. Stir in porcini and thyme. Sprinkle flour over onion mixture; cook 1 minute, stirring. Whisk in milk, mushroom liquid, nutmeg, salt, and pepper. Heat to boiling over medium-high heat; cook 2 to 3 minutes or until mixture thickens slightly, stirring frequently.

4   Add porcini sauce to pasta. Stir in Fontina, ricotta, and ½ cup Parmesan. Spoon pasta into 3-quart ceramic baking dish; sprinkle with remaining Parmesan. Bake 30 minutes or until center is hot and top is golden.

EACH SERVING: ABOUT 465 CALORIES | 24G PROTEIN | 55G CARBOHYDRATE | 16G TOTAL FAT (8G SATURATED) | 42MG CHOLESTEROL | 765MG SODIUM

GREEK PASTA BOWL WITH SHRIMP

Oregano and feta cheese—two staples of Greek cooking—flavor this dish. For an even speedier prep time, substitute preshelled and deveined frozen raw shrimp for the fresh.

ACTIVE TIME: 15 MINUTES · **TOTAL TIME:** 30 MINUTES
MAKES: 6 MAIN-DISH SERVINGS

1 PACKAGE (16 OUNCES) GEMELLI OR FUSILLI PASTA

2 TABLESPOONS OLIVE OIL

1 POUND MEDIUM SHRIMP, SHELLED AND DEVEINED

2 GARLIC CLOVES, CRUSHED WITH GARLIC PRESS

1 TABLESPOON FRESH OREGANO LEAVES, MINCED, OR ½ TEASPOON DRIED OREGANO

½ TEASPOON SALT

¼ TEASPOON GROUND BLACK PEPPER

2 BUNCHES GREEN ONIONS, THINLY SLICED

3 MEDIUM TOMATOES (1 POUND), COARSELY CHOPPED

2 PACKAGES (4 OUNCES EACH) CRUMBLED FETA CHEESE (2 CUPS)

FRESH OREGANO SPRIGS FOR GARNISH

1 In large saucepot, cook pasta as label directs.

2 Meanwhile, in 12-inch skillet, heat oil over medium-high heat until hot. Add shrimp, garlic, oregano, salt, and pepper and cook 1 minute, stirring. Add green onions and cook 2 minutes or just until shrimp turn opaque throughout. Stir in tomatoes.

3 Drain pasta; return to saucepot. Add shrimp mixture and feta; toss well to combine. Garnish each serving with the fresh oregano sprigs.

EACH SERVING: ABOUT 515 CALORIES | 29G PROTEIN | 65G CARBOHYDRATE | 15G TOTAL FAT (7G SATURATED) | 127MG CHOLESTEROL | 815MG SODIUM

TUNA-MELT CASSEROLE

If you enjoy diner tuna-melt sandwiches, you'll love this. We've added tomatoes and broccoli for extra flavor, color, and vitamins.

ACTIVE TIME: 40 MINUTES · **TOTAL TIME:** 1 HOUR

MAKES: 6 MAIN-DISH SERVINGS

1   PACKAGE (16 OUNCES) CORKSCREW OR MEDIUM SHELL PASTA

3   CUPS BROCCOLI FLORETS

2   TABLESPOONS BUTTER OR MARGARINE

2   TABLESPOONS ALL-PURPOSE FLOUR

¾   TEASPOON SALT

¼   TEASPOON COARSELY GROUND BLACK PEPPER

4   CUPS REDUCED-FAT (2%) MILK

4   OUNCES SWISS CHEESE, SHREDDED (1 CUP)

1   CAN (12 OUNCES) CHUNK LIGHT TUNA IN WATER, DRAINED AND FLAKED

2   MEDIUM TOMATOES, CUT INTO ¼-INCH-THICK SLICES

1   Preheat oven to 400°F. In large saucepot, cook pasta in boiling *salted water* 5 minutes; add broccoli to pasta and cook another 5 minutes or until broccoli is tender and pasta is al dente. Drain well and return to saucepot; set aside.

2   Meanwhile, in 3-quart saucepan, melt butter over low heat. Stir in flour, salt, and pepper until blended and cook, stirring, 1 minute. Gradually stir in milk; increase heat to medium-high and cook, stirring occasionally, until mixture thickens and boils. Boil 1 minute, stirring frequently. Remove saucepan from heat and stir in ½ cup Swiss cheese until blended.

3   Add cheese sauce and tuna to pasta and broccoli in saucepot; toss until evenly mixed. Transfer mixture to shallow 3½-quart casserole or 13" by 9" glass baking dish. Arrange tomato slices on top, overlapping if necessary. Sprinkle with remaining ½ cup cheese.

4   Cover baking dish with foil and bake 20 minutes or until hot and bubbly.

EACH SERVING: ABOUT 570 CALORIES | 39G PROTEIN | 71G CARBOHYDRATE | 14G TOTAL FAT (6G SATURATED) | 29MG CHOLESTEROL | 755MG SODIUM

SALMON NOODLE BAKE

This updated tuna noodle casserole is loaded with chunks of fresh salmon and flavored with leeks, mushrooms, and herbs.

ACTIVE TIME: 25 MINUTES · **TOTAL TIME:** 45 MINUTES
MAKES: 6 MAIN-DISH SERVINGS

1½ CUPS LOW-FAT (1%) MILK

1 LARGE LEEK (1 POUND)

10 OUNCES SLICED MUSHROOMS

1 TABLESPOON REDUCED-SODIUM SOY SAUCE

2 TABLESPOONS PLUS 1 TEASPOON OLIVE OIL

2 LARGE STALKS CELERY, FINELY CHOPPED

2 TEASPOONS CHOPPED FRESH THYME LEAVES

3 TABLESPOONS ALL-PURPOSE FLOUR

1 CAN (14½ OUNCES) REDUCED-SODIUM CHICKEN BROTH (1¾ CUPS)

8 OUNCES CURLY EGG NOODLES

12 OUNCES SKINLESS SALMON FILLET, CUT INTO 1-INCH CHUNKS

1 CUP FROZEN PEAS

½ TEASPOON SALT

¼ TEASPOON GROUND BLACK PEPPER

⅓ CUP PANKO (JAPANESE-STYLE BREAD CRUMBS)

1 TABLESPOON CHOPPED FRESH FLAT-LEAF PARSLEY LEAVES FOR GARNISH

1 Preheat oven to 350°F. Grease 3-quart shallow baking dish. Heat large covered saucepot of *water* to boiling over high heat. In glass measuring cup, microwave milk on High 2 minutes or until warm.

2 Meanwhile, trim and discard root and dark green top from leek. Discard tough outer leaves. Cut leek lengthwise in half, then crosswise into ¼-inch-wide slices. Place leek in bowl of cold water; with hand, swish to remove sand. Remove leek to colander. Repeat process with fresh water, changing water several times until sand is removed. Drain leek and set aside.

3 In 12-inch skillet, combine mushrooms and soy sauce. Cook 5 to 6 minutes over medium-high heat until mushrooms are tender and sauce evaporates, stirring occasionally. Transfer to large bowl.

4 In same skillet, heat 2 tablespoons oil over medium-high heat. Add leek, celery, and 1 teaspoon thyme. Cook 2 minutes or until golden and just tender, stirring. Add flour and cook 1 minute, stirring. Stir in broth, then milk, in steady stream. Heat to boiling, stirring; then cook 2 minutes or until thickened, stirring constantly. Transfer to bowl with mushrooms.

5 While sauce cooks, add noodles to pot filled with boiling water; cook 1 minute. Drain well.

6 To bowl with mushroom mixture, add noodles, salmon, frozen peas, salt, and pepper. Gently stir to combine. Spread mixture in prepared dish.

7 In small bowl, combine panko and remaining 1 teaspoon each thyme and oil. Sprinkle evenly over top of noodle mixture. Bake 17 to 18 minutes or until topping turns golden brown. Garnish with chopped parsley.

EACH SERVING: ABOUT 370 CALORIES | 22G PROTEIN | 43G CARBOHYDRATE | 12G TOTAL FAT (2G SATURATED) | 61MG CHOLESTEROL | 570MG SODIUM ☺

BAKED PASTA WITH BUTTERNUT SQUASH

To save some prep time for this recipe, look for cut-up butternut squash in your produce department.

ACTIVE TIME: 45 MINUTES · **TOTAL TIME:** 1 HOUR 15 MINUTES
MAKES: 6 MAIN-DISH SERVINGS

---

4 OUNCES PANCETTA, CUT INTO ¼-INCH PIECES

5 SHALLOTS, SLICED (1 CUP)

¼ TEASPOON GROUND BLACK PEPPER

2 TEASPOONS OLIVE OIL

1 BUTTERNUT SQUASH (2 POUNDS), PEELED, SEEDED, AND CUT INTO ¾-INCH CHUNKS

1 CONTAINER (10 OUNCES) BRUSSELS SPROUTS, EACH CUT INTO QUARTERS

10 MEDIUM SAGE LEAVES, CHOPPED (3 TABLESPOONS)

1 CAN (14 TO 14½ OUNCES) CHICKEN BROTH (1¾ CUPS)

1 PACKAGE (16 OUNCES) CAVATAPPI OR CORKSCREW PASTA

1½ CUPS REDUCED-FAT (2%) MILK

1 CUP FRESHLY GRATED PARMESAN CHEESE (3 OUNCES)

¼ CUP PLAIN DRIED BREAD CRUMBS

FRIED SAGE LEAVES (RECIPE FOLLOWS) FOR GARNISH

1 Preheat oven to 375°F. In nonstick 12-inch skillet, cook pancetta over medium heat about 10 minutes or until browned, stirring occasionally. With slotted spoon, transfer pancetta to medium bowl. In same skillet, cook shallots with pepper about 5 minutes or until golden, stirring frequently. Transfer shallots to bowl with pancetta.

2 In same skillet, heat oil over medium heat until hot; add squash and cook, covered, 10 minutes, stirring often. Add Brussels sprouts, sage, and broth; cook, covered, 10 to 12 minutes or until vegetables are tender and most of liquid is absorbed.

3 Meanwhile, in large saucepot, cook pasta 2 minutes less than label directs. Drain and return to saucepot.

4 Stir milk into skillet with squash and heat through. Add squash mixture, pancetta mixture, and ¾ cup Parmesan to pasta in saucepot; toss until well mixed. Spoon pasta into 3-quart ceramic baking dish and sprinkle with bread crumbs and remaining ¼ cup Parmesan. Bake 30 minutes or until center is hot and top is golden.

5 Meanwhile, prepare Fried Sage Leaves. Garnish baked pasta with Fried Sage Leaves to serve.

FRIED SAGE LEAVES

Heat ¼ **cup olive oil** in 10-inch skillet over medium heat until hot. Add ½ **cup sage leaves,** rinsed and patted dry; cook about 1 minute or until crisp, turning leaves over once and being careful not to burn them. Remove with slotted spoon; drain on paper towels.

EACH SERVING: ABOUT 600 CALORIES | 25G PROTEIN | 87G CARBOHYDRATE | 17G TOTAL FAT (8G SATURATED) | 27MG CHOLESTEROL | 760MG SODIUM 📷

VEGGIE MAC 'N' CHEESE

This take on a homestyle favorite adds broccoli, cauliflower, and green peas to the usual mix of plain pasta and gooey Cheddar cheese. The result: a great dish for vegetarians or kids who have a tough time getting their recommended daily servings of veggies. For photo, see page 66.

ACTIVE TIME: 20 MINUTES · **TOTAL TIME:** 35 MINUTES
MAKES: 6 MAIN-DISH SERVINGS

12 OUNCES ROTINI PASTA	2 TABLESPOONS BUTTER OR MARGARINE
8 OUNCES SMALL BROCCOLI FLORETS	
12 OUNCES SMALL CAULIFLOWER FLORETS	½ TEASPOON MUSTARD POWDER
	⅛ TEASPOON GROUND NUTMEG
1 CUP FROZEN PEAS	⅛ TEASPOON CAYENNE (GROUND RED) PEPPER
12 OUNCES REDUCED-FAT EXTRA-SHARP CHEDDAR, SHREDDED (3 CUPS)	
	¼ TEASPOON SALT
8 OUNCES NEUFCHÂTEL CHEESE	3 CUPS REDUCED-FAT (2%) MILK

1 Preheat oven to 400°F. Grease six 16-ounce casserole dishes (or one 3-quart shallow baking dish).

2 Heat large covered saucepot of *salted water* to boiling over high heat. Add pasta; cook 3 minutes, uncovered. Add broccoli, cauliflower, and frozen peas; cook 1 minute. Drain well.

3 Meanwhile, in food processor with knife blade attached, pulse 8 ounces Cheddar (2 cups), cream cheese, butter, mustard powder, nutmeg, cayenne pepper, and salt until well blended. With processor running, add milk. Puree until smooth.

4 Return pasta mixture to saucepot and immediately add milk mixture. Stir well to evenly coat. Divide evenly among prepared casseroles or pour into prepared baking dish. Top with remaining Cheddar.

5 Place dishes on jelly-roll pan and bake uncovered 15 to 20 minutes or until just bubbling. (If using 3-quart dish, cover tightly with foil and bake 20 minutes. Uncover and bake 10 minutes longer.)

EACH SERVING: ABOUT 620 CALORIES | 33G PROTEIN | 60G CARBOHYDRATE | 28G TOTAL FAT (15G SATURATED) | 78MG CHOLESTEROL | 840MG SODIUM

PEPPERONI RIGATONI BAKE

This simple, hearty dish will warm you up on a cold night.

ACTIVE TIME: 25 MINUTES · **TOTAL TIME:** 45 MINUTES
MAKES: 6 MAIN-DISH SERVINGS

1   PACKAGE (16 OUNCES) RIGATONI OR PENNE PASTA

2   LARGE EGGS

1   CUP WHOLE MILK

1   CUP SHREDDED PART-SKIM MOZZARELLA CHEESE (4 OUNCES)

1   CUP GRATED PARMESAN CHEESE (3 OUNCES)

1   CONTAINER (15 OUNCES) PART-SKIM RICOTTA CHEESE

4   OUNCES SLICED PEPPERONI, CUT INTO SLIVERS (1 CUP)

1   PACKAGE (10 OUNCES) FROZEN PEAS

½   TEASPOON SALT

¼   TEASPOON GROUND BLACK PEPPER

1   Heat large covered saucepot of *salted water* to boiling over high heat. Add rigatoni and cook as label directs.

2   Meanwhile, preheat oven to 375°F. Grease 3- to 3½-quart casserole (about 2 inches deep) or 13" by 9" glass baking dish.

3   In large bowl, with wire whisk, lightly beat eggs. Stir in milk, mozzarella, Parmesan, ricotta, pepperoni slivers, frozen peas, salt, and pepper until well combined.

4   Drain rigatoni. Add rigatoni to cheese mixture and toss to coat. Transfer pasta and cheese mixture to prepared casserole. Bake, uncovered, 20 to 25 minutes or until edges are golden and center is almost set. Let stand 5 minutes before serving.

EACH SERVING: ABOUT 675 CALORIES | 39G PROTEIN | 70G CARBOHYDRATE | 26G TOTAL FAT (13G SATURATED) | 4G FIBER | 134MG CHOLESTEROL | 1,280MG SODIUM

SPAGHETTI PIE WITH PROSCIUTTO AND PEAS

For a healthy twist, try making this with whole-wheat spaghetti.

ACTIVE TIME: 25 MINUTES · **TOTAL TIME:** 40 MINUTES
MAKES: 6 MAIN-DISH SERVINGS

8	OUNCES THICK SPAGHETTI	¼	TEASPOON SALT
4	LARGE EGGS	¼	TEASPOON GROUND BLACK PEPPER
2	LARGE EGG WHITES	1	TABLESPOON BUTTER OR MARGARINE
1	CONTAINER (15 OUNCES) PART-SKIM RICOTTA CHEESE	1	BUNCH GREEN ONIONS, CUT INTO ¼-INCH PIECES (1 CUP)
¾	CUP REDUCED-FAT (2%) MILK	1	CUP FROZEN PEAS
⅛	TEASPOON GROUND NUTMEG	6	THIN SLICES PROSCIUTTO (3 OUNCES)

---

1 Preheat oven to 350°F. In large saucepot, cook spaghetti 2 minutes less than label directs.

2 Meanwhile, in medium bowl, whisk eggs, egg whites, ricotta, milk, nutmeg, salt, and pepper until blended. Set aside. In oven-safe nonstick 12-inch skillet, melt butter over medium heat. Add green onions and cook about 5 minutes or until softened. Remove skillet from heat.

3 Drain spaghetti. To green onions in skillet, add spaghetti and frozen peas; toss to combine. Pour egg mixture over pasta and arrange prosciutto slices on top.

4 Place skillet over medium-high heat and cook 3 to 5 minutes or until edges just begin to set. Place skillet in oven and bake 15 minutes or until center is set. Slide pie onto large plate to serve.

EACH SERVING: ABOUT 375 CALORIES | 25G PROTEIN | 38G CARBOHYDRATE | 13G TOTAL FAT (6G SATURATED) | 175MG CHOLESTEROL | 700MG SODIUM ☺

BEEF AND SAUSAGE LASAGNA

This crowd-pleasing lasagna layers noodles with a spicy sausage and beef sauce, ricotta, and plenty of mozzarella.

ACTIVE TIME: 1 HOUR · **TOTAL TIME:** 1 HOUR 45 MINUTES
MAKES: 10 MAIN-DISH SERVINGS

8	OUNCES HOT ITALIAN-SAUSAGE LINKS, CASINGS REMOVED	1	CONTAINER (15 OUNCES) PART-SKIM RICOTTA CHEESE
8	OUNCES GROUND BEEF CHUCK	1	LARGE EGG
1	ONION, CHOPPED	¼	CUP CHOPPED FRESH PARSLEY
1	CAN (28 OUNCES) PLUM TOMATOES IN JUICE	⅛	TEASPOON COARSELY GROUND BLACK PEPPER
2	TABLESPOONS TOMATO PASTE	8	OUNCES PART-SKIM MOZZARELLA CHEESE, SHREDDED (2 CUPS)
1¼	TEASPOONS SALT		
12	LASAGNA NOODLES (10 OUNCES)		

1 In 4-quart saucepan, cook sausage, ground beef, and onion over high heat, breaking up sausage and meat with side of spoon, until meat is well browned. Discard fat. Add tomatoes with their juice, tomato paste, and 1 teaspoon salt. Heat to boiling, breaking up tomatoes with side of spoon. Reduce heat; cover and simmer, stirring occasionally, 30 minutes.

2 Meanwhile, in large saucepot, cook lasagna noodles as label directs but do not add salt to water. Drain and rinse with cold running water. Return to saucepot with enough *cold water* to cover.

3 Preheat oven to 375°F. In medium bowl, stir ricotta, egg, parsley, remaining ¼ teaspoon salt, and pepper until well combined.

4 Drain noodles and spread them out on clean kitchen towels. In 13" by 9" baking dish, arrange 6 lasagna noodles, overlapping to fit. Spread with all of ricotta mixture and sprinkle with half of mozzarella; top with half of meat sauce. Cover with remaining 6 noodles and spread with remaining meat sauce. Sprinkle with remaining mozzarella.

5 Cover lasagna with foil and bake 30 minutes. Remove foil and bake until sauce is bubbling and top has lightly browned, about 15 minutes longer. Let stand 15 minutes for easier serving.

EACH SERVING: ABOUT 365 CALORIES | 23G PROTEIN | 31G CARBOHYDRATE | 16G TOTAL FAT (7G SATURATED) | 74MG CHOLESTEROL | 780MG SODIUM ☺ 🍴

PERFECT LASAGNA

Preparing lasagna is time-intensive, but well worth the effort. For mouthwatering results, follow these guidelines.

- Be sure to brown the meat well and discard excess fat before adding the tomatoes. Simmer until the sauce is thick; excess liquid will make your lasagna soupy.

- To ensure the noodles don't overcook (or stick together), drain and rinse them with cold water, then return them to the pot and cover with cold water until it's time to assemble the lasagna.

- When assembling the layers, be sure to divide the ingredients equally between the layers and spread them evenly over the entire lasagna, so there will be meat sauce, ricotta, and mozzarella in every bite.

- Always let the lasagna stand for a good fifteen minutes after baking so the ingredients have time to settle—it makes for easier cutting.

SUMMERY VEGETABLE TART

Refrigerated ready-to-unroll piecrust is the shortcut secret to this pretty savory tart. Slathered with basil cream cheese, it's filled with squash, red peppers, and zucchini.

ACTIVE TIME: 25 MINUTES · **TOTAL TIME:** 1 HOUR 5 MINUTES
MAKES: 4 MAIN-DISH SERVINGS

1   TABLESPOON PLUS 1 TEASPOON EXTRA-VIRGIN OLIVE OIL

1   GARLIC CLOVE, CRUSHED WITH GARLIC PRESS

1   SMALL RED ONION, FINELY CHOPPED

1   LARGE RED PEPPER, FINELY CHOPPED

¼   TEASPOON SALT

¼   TEASPOON GROUND BLACK PEPPER

4   OUNCES CREAM CHEESE, SOFTENED

¼   CUP FRESH BASIL LEAVES, FINELY CHOPPED, PLUS ADDITIONAL FOR GARNISH

1   SMALL ZUCCHINI (4 OUNCES), TRIMMED

1   SMALL YELLOW SQUASH (4 OUNCES), TRIMMED

1   (9-INCH) REFRIGERATED PIECRUST, READY-TO-UNROLL

1   Preheat oven to 425°F.

2   In 12-inch skillet, heat 1 tablespoon oil over medium-high heat. Add garlic and cook 30 seconds, stirring. Add onion, red pepper, and ⅛ teaspoon each salt and black pepper. Cook 4 minutes or until softened and browned, stirring frequently. Remove from heat and let cool to room temperature. Mixture can be refrigerated, covered, up to overnight.

3   While mixture cools, combine cream cheese, basil, and ⅛ teaspoon each salt and pepper; stir until well mixed. With vegetable peeler, peel zucchini and squash lengthwise into thin ribbons (see Tip).

4   Lay piecrust flat on jelly-roll pan. Spread cream cheese mixture in even layer, leaving 1-inch border. Spread onion-pepper mixture over cream cheese; decoratively arrange zucchini and squash ribbons on top. Fold border of dough over vegetable mixture. Brush remaining 1 teaspoon oil over zucchini and squash.

5   Bake 30 to 35 minutes or until edges of crust are browned. Serve tart warm or at room temperature.

TIP   Make pretty zucchini and squash ribbons using a vegetable peeler: If the vegetables have a lot of seeds, rotate them 90 degrees each time you hit the seeds, and start peeling on a different side. Discard the core of seeds.

EACH SERVING: ABOUT 395 CALORIES | 5G PROTEIN | 34G CARBOHYDRATE | 29G TOTAL FAT (12G SATURATED) | 37MG CHOLESTEROL | 520MG SODIUM ☺ 🍴

BACON AND CHEESE STRATA

You can assemble this brunch-worthy casserole a day ahead, then pop it in the oven right from the refrigerator.

ACTIVE TIME: 30 MINUTES · **TOTAL TIME:** 1 HOUR 5 MINUTES PLUS STANDING

MAKES: 6 MAIN-DISH SERVINGS

---

6 SLICES BACON	9 LARGE EGGS
2 TABLESPOONS DIJON MUSTARD WITH SEEDS	3 CUPS WHOLE MILK
12 SLICES FIRM WHITE BREAD	½ TEASPOON SALT
6 OUNCES GRUYÈRE CHEESE, SHREDDED (1½ CUPS)	¼ TEASPOON GROUND BLACK PEPPER

1 On microwave-safe plate, place bacon on double thickness of paper towels and cover with 1 paper towel. Cook on High 2 to 3 minutes or until browned. Let stand 5 minutes or until cool and crisp. Coarsely crumble bacon.

2 Meanwhile, grease 13" by 9" ceramic or glass baking dish.

3 Spread mustard on one side of each slice of bread. Arrange 6 bread slices, mustard side up, in bottom half of baking dish, cutting slices to fit if necessary. Sprinkle with half of cheese. Top with all but 2 tablespoons crumbled bacon, then remaining bread slices, mustard side up.

4 In large bowl, with wire whisk, beat eggs, milk, salt, and pepper until blended. Slowly pour egg mixture over bread slices; press bread down to help it absorb egg mixture. If necessary, spoon egg mixture over any uncoated bread. Top with remaining cheese and bacon. Let stand at room temperature 15 minutes or cover and refrigerate overnight.

5 Preheat oven to 350°F. Bake strata 40 minutes or until puffed and golden; knife inserted in center should come out clean. Let stand 10 minutes before serving.

EACH SERVING: ABOUT 480 CALORIES | 28G PROTEIN | 32G CARBOHYDRATE | 26G TOTAL FAT (12G SATURATED) | 372MG CHOLESTEROL | 840MG SODIUM

POTATO-CRUSTED QUICHE

It's much easier to get clean slices for this egg-based dish if you spread the potatoes very thinly, without any empty patches. This will prevent the egg mixture from sticking to the pan.

ACTIVE TIME: 20 MINUTES · **TOTAL TIME:** 40 MINUTES

MAKES: 4 MAIN-DISH SERVINGS

4	LARGE EGGS	2	GREEN ONIONS, CHOPPED
1	LARGE EGG WHITE	2	TABLESPOONS OLIVE OIL
1⅔	CUPS LOW-FAT (1%) MILK	2	OUNCES GRUYÈRE CHEESE, SHREDDED
¼	TEASPOON SALT	2	PLUM TOMATOES, THINLY SLICED
⅛	TEASPOON FRESHLY GROUND BLACK PEPPER		THINLY SLICED FRESH FLAT-LEAF PARSLEY LEAVES FOR GARNISH
4	OUNCES HAM, CUT INTO ¼-INCH PIECES		SNIPPED FRESH CHIVES FOR GARNISH
1½	POUNDS POTATOES, PEELED AND SHREDDED		

1 Preheat oven to 375°F.

2 In large bowl, with wire whisk, blend eggs, egg white, milk, and ⅛ teaspoon each salt and pepper. Stir in ham. Set aside.

3 Place potatoes in large fine-mesh sieve. With hands, squeeze out as much liquid as possible. Transfer to large bowl and toss with green onions and remaining ⅛ teaspoon salt.

4 Heat 12-inch well-seasoned plain or enamel-coated cast-iron skillet on medium-high until hot. Add oil and heat until very hot, brushing to evenly coat bottom and side. Add potatoes; with rubber spatula, quickly spread in thin, even layer over bottom and all the way up side to rim, gently pressing potatoes against pan to form a crust. Patch any holes by using spatula to spread potatoes over them. Cook 3 minutes or until browned. Pour in egg mixture, then sprinkle cheese evenly over top.

5 Bake 15 to 20 minutes or until a knife inserted in center comes out clean. Decoratively arrange tomato slices on top. Garnish with parsley and chives. Use thin spatula to release sides of crust from pan, then cut into wedges to serve.

EACH SERVING: ABOUT 425 CALORIES | 23G PROTEIN | 39G CARBOHYDRATE | 20G TOTAL FAT (6G SATURATED) | 253MG CHOLESTEROL | 660MG SODIUM ☺

TOMATO-CHEESE PIE

A savory custard pie that bakes right in the pie plate—with no crust!

ACTIVE TIME: 20 MINUTES · **TOTAL TIME:** 50 MINUTES

MAKES: 6 MAIN-DISH SERVINGS

---

1   CONTAINER (15 OUNCES) PART-SKIM RICOTTA CHEESE

4   LARGE EGGS

¼   CUP GRATED PARMESAN CHEESE

¾   TEASPOON SALT PLUS ADDITIONAL FOR SPRINKLING

⅛   TEASPOON COARSELY GROUND BLACK PEPPER PLUS ADDITIONAL FOR SPRINKLING

¼   CUP LOW-FAT (1%) MILK

1   TABLESPOON CORNSTARCH

1   CUP PACKED FRESH BASIL LEAVES, CHOPPED

1   POUND RIPE TOMATOES (3 MEDIUM), THINLY SLICED

1 Preheat oven to 375°F. In large bowl, with wire whisk or fork, beat ricotta, eggs, Parmesan, salt, and pepper until blended.

2 In cup, stir milk and cornstarch until smooth; whisk into cheese mixture. Stir in basil.

3 Pour mixture into 9-inch glass or ceramic pie plate. Arrange tomatoes on top, overlapping if necessary. Sprinkle tomatoes with salt and pepper. Bake pie 30 to 35 minutes or until lightly browned around edge and center is puffed.

EACH SERVING: ABOUT 190 CALORIES | 15G PROTEIN | 10G CARBOHYDRATE | 10G TOTAL FAT (5G SATURATED) | 167MG CHOLESTEROL | 515MG SODIUM ☺

CHILI POTPIE WITH BISCUIT CRUST

Cornmeal-and-Cheddar biscuit crust makes a homey topper for spicy beef chili filling.

ACTIVE TIME: 30 MINUTES · TOTAL TIME: 2 HOURS 15 MINUTES
MAKES: 6 MAIN-DISH SERVINGS

- 1 TABLESPOON PLUS 3 TEASPOONS OLIVE OIL
- 1 POUND BONELESS BEEF CHUCK, CUT INTO ½-INCH PIECES
- 1 ONION, CHOPPED
- 2 GARLIC CLOVES, MINCED
- 1 TABLESPOON CHILI POWDER
- 1 TEASPOON GROUND CORIANDER
- ½ TEASPOON SALT
- ½ TEASPOON GROUND CUMIN
- 1 CAN (16 OUNCES) WHOLE TOMATOES IN PUREE

- 1 CAN (4 TO 4½ OUNCES) CHOPPED MILD GREEN CHILES
- 1 TABLESPOON DARK BROWN SUGAR
- 1 TABLESPOON TOMATO PASTE
- ¼ CUP WATER
- 1 CAN (15 TO 16 OUNCES) PINK BEANS
- ¼ CUP CHOPPED FRESH CILANTRO LEAVES
- CHEDDAR-BISCUIT CRUST (RECIPE FOLLOWS)
- 2 TEASPOONS MILK
- GREEN ONIONS FOR GARNISH (OPTIONAL)

1 In 5-quart Dutch oven or saucepot, heat 1 tablespoon oil over medium-high heat until hot. Add half the beef and cook until browned and juices evaporate. Transfer beef to small bowl. Repeat with remaining beef and 2 teaspoons oil.

2 Add remaining 1 teaspoon oil to Dutch oven. Reduce heat to medium. Add onion and cook 10 minutes or until tender and golden. Add garlic; cook 2 minutes, stirring. Add chili powder, coriander, salt, and cumin; cook 1 minute, stirring.

3 Add tomatoes with their puree, breaking up tomatoes with side of spoon. Add chiles with their juice, brown sugar, tomato paste, beef with any accumulated juices in bowl, and water; heat to boiling over high heat. Reduce heat to low; cover and simmer 30 minutes, stirring occasionally.

4 Rinse and drain beans. Add beans to Dutch oven; heat to boiling over high heat. Reduce heat to low; cover and simmer 30 to 45 minutes longer, until beef is very tender. Stir in cilantro.

5 Preheat oven to 425°F. Meanwhile, prepare Cheddar-Biscuit Crust.

6 Spoon hot chili mixture into deep 2-quart casserole or 9-inch deep-dish pie plate. Top with biscuit crust, tucking in edge to fit. With tip of knife, cut out 5 oval openings in crust to allow steam to escape during baking. (Do not just make slits; they will close up as crust bakes.) Brush crust with milk to add shine.

7 Place sheet of foil underneath casserole; crimp foil edges to form a rim to catch any drips during baking. Bake pie 20 minutes or until crust is browned. Cool slightly.

8 Garnish each serving with green onions if you like.

CHEDDAR-BISCUIT CRUST

In medium bowl, mix **1 cup all-purpose flour**, ⅓ **cup shredded sharp Cheddar cheese**, ¼ **cup yellow cornmeal**, **2 teaspoons baking powder**, and ½ **teaspoon salt.** With pastry blender or 2 knives used scissor-fashion, cut in **3 tablespoons cold butter or margarine** until mixture resembles coarse crumbs. Stir in ½ **cup milk;** quickly mix just until a soft dough forms and leaves side of bowl. Turn dough onto lightly floured surface; gently knead about 5 strokes to mix thoroughly. With floured rolling pin, roll dough into a round 1 inch larger in diameter than top of casserole.

EACH SERVING: ABOUT 515 CALORIES | 24G PROTEIN | 45G CARBOHYDRATE | 27G TOTAL FAT (8G SATURATED) | 58MG CHOLESTEROL | 1,320MG SODIUM ▭

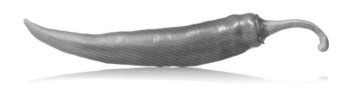

TURKEY POTPIE WITH CORNMEAL CRUST

Treat your family to the ultimate in comfort food—tender turkey and veggies in a velvety sauce nestled under a golden crust.

ACTIVE TIME: 30 MINUTES · **TOTAL TIME:** 1 HOUR 5 MINUTES
MAKES: 10 MAIN-DISH SERVINGS

- 1 TABLESPOON VEGETABLE OIL
- 1 RUTABAGA (1 POUND), PEELED AND CUT INTO ½-INCH PIECES
- 3 CARROTS, PEELED AND CUT INTO ½-INCH PIECES
- 1 LARGE ONION (12 OUNCES), CHOPPED
- 1 POUND ALL-PURPOSE POTATOES (3 MEDIUM), PEELED AND CUT INTO ½-INCH PIECES
- 2 LARGE STALKS CELERY, CHOPPED
- ¾ TEASPOON SALT
- 1 POUND COOKED TURKEY OR CHICKEN, CUT INTO ½-INCH PIECES (4 CUPS)
- 1 PACKAGE (10 OUNCES) FROZEN PEAS
- 1 CAN (14½ OUNCES) CHICKEN BROTH
- 1 CUP MILK
- ¼ CUP ALL-PURPOSE FLOUR
- ¼ TEASPOON GROUND BLACK PEPPER
- ⅛ TEASPOON DRIED THYME
- CORNMEAL CRUST (RECIPE FOLLOWS)
- 1 LARGE EGG, BEATEN

1 In 12-inch skillet, heat oil over medium-high heat; add rutabaga, carrots, and onion and cook 10 minutes. Stir in potatoes, celery, and ½ teaspoon salt; cook, stirring frequently, until rutabaga is tender-crisp, about 10 minutes longer. Spoon into 13" by 9" baking dish; add turkey and frozen peas.
2 In 2-quart saucepan, heat broth to boiling. Meanwhile, in small bowl, blend milk and flour until smooth. Stir milk mixture into broth; add pepper, thyme, and remaining ¼ teaspoon salt. Heat to boiling over high heat, stirring. Stir sauce into turkey-vegetable mixture in baking dish.
3 Prepare Cornmeal Crust. Preheat oven to 425°F.
4 On lightly floured surface, with floured rolling pin, roll dough into rectangle 4 inches larger than top of baking dish. Arrange dough rectangle over filling; trim edge, leaving 1-inch overhang. Fold overhang under; flute. Brush crust with some egg. If desired, reroll trimmings; cut into decorative shapes to garnish top of pie. Brush dough cutouts with egg. Cut several slits in crust to allow steam to escape during baking.
5 Place potpie on foil-lined baking sheet to catch any overflow during baking. Bake potpie until crust is golden brown and filling is hot and bubbling, 35 to 40 minutes. During last 10 minutes of baking, cover edges of crust with foil to prevent overbrowning.

CORNMEAL CRUST

In large bowl, combine 1½ **cups all-purpose flour, ¼ cup cornmeal,** and ¾ **teaspoon salt.** With pastry blender or 2 knives used scissor-fashion, cut in ⅔ **cup vegetable shortening** until mixture resembles coarse crumbs. Sprinkle **6 to 7 tablespoons cold water,** 1 tablespoon at a time, over flour mixture, mixing with fork after each addition until dough is just moist enough to hold together.

EACH SERVING: ABOUT 415 CALORIES | 21G PROTEIN | 42G CARBOHYDRATE | 18G TOTAL FAT (5G SATURATED) | 60MG CHOLESTEROL | 644MG SODIUM 😊 🍲

TAMALE PIE

Enjoy the great taste of tamales with less work. A green salad with grapefruit sections and sliced avocado makes a nice accompaniment.

ACTIVE TIME: 30 MINUTES · **TOTAL TIME:** 1 HOUR 10 MINUTES
MAKES: 6 MAIN-DISH SERVINGS

2	TEASPOONS VEGETABLE OIL	1	CAN (15¼ TO 16 OUNCES) WHOLE-KERNEL CORN, DRAINED
1	ONION, CHOPPED		
1	POUND GROUND BEEF CHUCK	4	CUPS WATER
1	TABLESPOON CHILI POWDER	1	CUP CORNMEAL
1	TEASPOON GROUND CUMIN	1	TEASPOON SALT
1	CUP MEDIUM-HOT SALSA	2	OUNCES CHEDDAR CHEESE, SHREDDED (½ CUP)

1 Preheat oven to 350°F. In nonstick 12-inch skillet, heat oil over medium; add onion and cook until tender and golden, 6 to 8 minutes. Stir in ground beef and cook, breaking up meat with side of spoon, until browned, 6 to 8 minutes. Skim and discard any fat. Stir in chili powder and cumin and cook 2 minutes longer. Remove from heat and stir in salsa and corn.

2 In 2-quart saucepan, heat water to boiling. With wire whisk, gradually whisk in cornmeal and salt. Cook over medium heat, whisking frequently, 5 minutes, until thickened.

3 Pour half of cornmeal mixture into shallow 2-quart casserole. Spoon beef mixture over cornmeal; spoon remaining cornmeal over beef and sprinkle Cheddar on top. Bake 45 minutes. Remove casserole from oven and let stand 15 to 25 minutes before serving.

TIP If you prefer firm slices, let the pie rest at least 25 minutes.

EACH SERVING: ABOUT 335 CALORIES | 21G PROTEIN | 33G CARBOHYDRATE | 13G TOTAL FAT (5G SATURATED) | 57MG CHOLESTEROL | 1,026 MG SODIUM ☺ ⬛

ARTICHOKE AND GOAT CHEESE PIZZA

Delicate layers of phyllo form the crust of this rich, savory pizza. If you will be using frozen phyllo, it's best to plan ahead. Leave the unwrapped package in the refrigerator for a full day. A gradual thaw will produce sheets that are pliable and less likely to stick together or tear.

ACTIVE TIME: 10 MINUTES · **TOTAL TIME:** 25 MINUTES
MAKES: 4 MAIN-DISH SERVINGS

6   SHEETS (16" BY 12" EACH) FRESH OR FROZEN (THAWED) PHYLLO

2   TABLESPOONS BUTTER OR MARGARINE, MELTED

4   OUNCES SOFT, MILD GOAT CHEESE, SUCH AS MONTRACHET

1   JAR (6 OUNCES) MARINATED ARTICHOKE HEARTS, DRAINED AND CUT INTO PIECES

1½ CUPS GRAPE OR CHERRY TOMATOES, EACH CUT IN HALF

1 Preheat oven to 450°F. Place 1 sheet of phyllo on ungreased large cookie sheet; brush with some melted butter. Repeat layering with remaining phyllo and butter, but do not brush top layer.

2 Crumble cheese over phyllo; top with artichokes and tomatoes. Bake until golden brown around edges, 12 to 15 minutes.

3 Transfer pizza to large cutting board. With pizza cutter or knife, cut pizza lengthwise in half, then cut each half crosswise into 4 pieces.

EACH SERVING (2 PIECES): ABOUT 240 CALORIES | 9G PROTEIN | 20G CARBOHYDRATE 16G TOTAL FAT (8G SATURATED) | 28MG CHOLESTEROL | 366MG SODIUM

OVEN DISHES

This chapter is chockfull of hearty fare that's sure to satisfy your family or a crowd. Casseroles like Indian chicken with rice require a minimum of prep. Our roasted chicken, pork loin, and braised lamb shanks with white beans are prepared with a medley of vegetables, so dinner is as easy as pulling the pan out of the oven. Looking for meat-free dinner options? Our Cabbage and Bulgur Casserole delivers veggie and whole-grain goodness in a single pan.

KEY TO ICONS

◔ 30 minutes or less   ♥ Heart healthy   ☺ Low calorie   🍲 Make ahead   🍲 Slow cooker

Pork Loin with Apples, Potatoes, and Sage (page 102)

POLENTA AND SAUSAGE CASSEROLE

Layers of creamy polenta, two cheeses, and a tomato-sausage sauce make this a terrific casserole for a potluck party, buffet, or brunch. The spicy, hearty sauce is also delicious on its own, served over pasta.

ACTIVE TIME: 1 HOUR · TOTAL TIME: 1 HOUR 35 MINUTES
MAKES: 8 MAIN-DISH SERVINGS

- 8 OUNCES SWEET ITALIAN-SAUSAGE LINKS, CASINGS REMOVED
- 8 OUNCES HOT ITALIAN-SAUSAGE LINKS, CASINGS REMOVED
- 1 TABLESPOON OLIVE OIL
- 1 LARGE ONION (12 OUNCES), CHOPPED
- 1 LARGE STALK CELERY, CHOPPED
- 1 CARROT, PEELED AND CHOPPED
- 1 CAN (28 OUNCES) PLUM TOMATOES IN PUREE
- 2 CUPS YELLOW CORNMEAL
- 1 CAN (14½ OUNCES) CHICKEN BROTH
- ¾ TEASPOON SALT
- 4½ CUPS BOILING WATER
- ½ CUP FRESHLY GRATED PARMESAN CHEESE
- 8 OUNCES FONTINA OR MOZZARELLA CHEESE, SHREDDED (2 CUPS)

1   Prepare tomato-sausage sauce: In nonreactive 5-quart Dutch oven, cook sweet and hot sausage meat over medium-high heat, breaking up meat with side of spoon, until browned. With slotted spoon, transfer meat to bowl. Discard fat from Dutch oven.

2   Add oil to Dutch oven. Add onion, celery, and carrot and cook over medium-high heat until browned. Stir in sausage and tomatoes with their puree, breaking up tomatoes with side of spoon. Heat to boiling over high heat. Reduce heat; cover Dutch oven and simmer 10 minutes. Remove cover and simmer 10 minutes longer.

3   Preheat oven to 350°F. Prepare polenta: In 4-quart saucepan, with wire whisk, mix cornmeal, broth, and salt. Over medium-high heat, add boiling water and cook, whisking constantly, until mixture has thickened, about 5 minutes. Whisk in Parmesan.

4   Grease 13" by 9" baking dish. Evenly spread half of polenta mixture in baking dish; top with half of tomato-sausage sauce, then half of Fontina. Repeat with remaining polenta mixture and sauce.

POLENTA 101

A staple of northern Italy, polenta is a mush made from cornmeal. Medium-ground cornmeal is the best choice for polenta; if possible, choose one that is water- or stone-ground, as both processes leave more of the bran and germ intact. Polenta can be eaten soft, with a little butter and cheese, or cooled until firm and cut into squares that may be fried or grilled. In the recipe opposite, we bake soft polenta in a casserole with a spicy tomato-sausage sauce.

Basic polenta is easy and quick to prepare; see step 3, opposite, for instructions. We've also discovered that polenta can be made with ease in the microwave. Here's how: In a deep 4-quart microwave-safe bowl or casserole, combine **2 cups low-fat milk, 1½ cups cornmeal,** and **1 teaspoon salt** until blended. Stir in **4½ cups boiling water.** Cook in microwave on High 12 to 15 minutes. After first 5 minutes, with wire whisk, stir vigorously until smooth (mixture will be lumpy at first). Stir two more times during cooking. When polenta is thick and creamy, stir in **4 tablespoons butter,** cut into pieces, and **½ cup freshly grated Parmesan cheese.** Makes 8 side-dish servings.

5 Bake casserole 15 minutes. Sprinkle with remaining Fontina; bake until mixture is bubbling and cheese is golden, about 20 minutes longer. Let stand 15 minutes for easier serving.

EACH SERVING: ABOUT 465 CALORIES | 23G PROTEIN | 38G CARBOHYDRATE | 25G TOTAL FAT (11G SATURATED) | 70MG CHOLESTEROL | 1,323MG SODIUM

LAMB SHANKS WITH BEANS AND ENDIVE

This hearty braise will warm you on the coldest of winter nights.

ACTIVE TIME: 1 HOUR 30 MINUTES · TOTAL TIME: 3 HOURS 30 MINUTES
MAKES: 8 MAIN-DISH SERVINGS

WHITE BEANS AND LAMB SHANKS

1 POUND DRY GREAT NORTHERN BEANS

8 SMALL LAMB SHANKS
(1 POUND EACH)

2½ TEASPOONS SALT

1 TEASPOON COARSELY GROUND
BLACK PEPPER

2 TABLESPOONS VEGETABLE OIL

6 GARLIC CLOVES, CRUSHED WITH SIDE
OF CHEF'S KNIFE

4 CARROTS, EACH PEELED AND CUT
INTO 1-INCH PIECES

1 LARGE ONION, COARSELY CHOPPED

¼ CUP ALL-PURPOSE FLOUR

2 TABLESPOONS TOMATO PASTE

2 CUPS DRY WHITE WINE

1 CAN (14 TO 14½ OUNCES) CHICKEN
BROTH (1¾ CUPS)

1 CUP WATER

2 SPRIGS FRESH ROSEMARY, PLUS
8 SPRIGS FOR GARNISH

ROASTED ENDIVE

1 TABLESPOON OLIVE OIL

½ TEASPOON SALT

¼ TEASPOON COARSELY GROUND
BLACK PEPPER

8 MEDIUM HEADS BELGIAN ENDIVE
(1½ POUNDS)

1 Prepare white beans: In 4-quart saucepan, place beans and enough *water* to cover by 2 inches; heat to boiling over high heat. Remove saucepan from heat; set aside 40 minutes to soften beans. Drain.

2 Meanwhile, prepare lamb shanks: Pat shanks dry with paper towels; sprinkle with 1 teaspoon salt and ½ teaspoon pepper. In 8-quart Dutch oven, heat oil over medium-high heat until very hot but not smoking. Add shanks, in batches, and cook 12 to 15 minutes, turning to brown all sides. Transfer shanks to large bowl as they brown. If necessary, reduce heat to medium before adding second batch of shanks to prevent over browning.

3 Preheat oven to 375°F. Add garlic, carrots, and onion to Dutch oven; cook 10 minutes or until browned and tender, stirring frequently. Add flour, tomato paste, and remaining 1½ teaspoons salt and ½ teaspoon pepper. Cook 2 minutes, stirring constantly. Add wine and heat to boiling, stirring until browned bits are loosened; boil 5 minutes. Add broth and water; heat to boiling. Stir in beans and 2 sprigs rosemary and return shanks to pot; heat to boiling. Cover Dutch oven and bake 1 hour.

4   Meanwhile, prepare roasted endive: In large bowl, with fork, mix oil, salt, and pepper. Trim root ends of endive and cut each head lengthwise in half. Toss endive with oil mixture to coat. In 15½" by 10½" jelly-roll pan, arrange endive, cut sides down.

5   After 1 hour, turn shanks over; replace cover. Place endive and shanks in same oven. Bake shanks and endive 1 hour or until meat is fork-tender and easily separates from bone and endive is very tender and bottoms begin to brown. (Instant-read thermometer inserted horizontally into shanks should register 145°F.)

6   When shanks are done, transfer to large bowl. Skim and discard fat from liquid. Remove and discard rosemary. To serve, onto each of 8 large dinner plates, spoon some beans and cooking liquid; top with a lamb shank and 2 endive halves. Garnish with a rosemary sprig.

EACH SERVING: ABOUT 755 CALORIES | 68G PROTEIN | 49G CARBOHYDRATE | 30G TOTAL FAT (11G SATURATED) | 198MG CHOLESTEROL | 1,155MG SODIUM

CARBONNADES À LA FLAMANDE

This Belgian standard makes a hearty cold-weather dinner. It should be prepared with a full-flavored dark beer to complement the sweet onions. But in a pinch, use lager. Serve over egg noodles.

ACTIVE TIME: 45 MINUTES · TOTAL TIME: 3 HOURS 15 MINUTES
MAKES: 8 MAIN-DISH SERVINGS

- 3 TABLESPOONS OLIVE OR VEGETABLE OIL
- 2 POUNDS ONIONS, THINLY SLICED
- 4 SLICES BACON, CHOPPED
- 3 POUNDS LEAN BONELESS BEEF CHUCK, TRIMMED AND CUT INTO 2-INCH PIECES
- ½ TEASPOON SALT
- ¼ TEASPOON GROUND BLACK PEPPER
- 3 TABLESPOONS ALL-PURPOSE FLOUR
- 1 CAN (14½ OUNCES) BEEF BROTH
- 1 BOTTLE (12 OUNCES) DARK BEER (NOT STOUT)
- ½ TEASPOON DRIED THYME
- 1 BAY LEAF

1   Preheat oven to 350°F. In 5-quart Dutch oven, heat 2 tablespoons oil over medium-high heat. Add onions and cook until tender and browned, 20 to 25 minutes. Transfer onions to large bowl.

2   In Dutch oven, cook bacon over medium heat until browned; with slotted spoon, transfer to bowl with onions.

3   Pat beef dry with paper towels; sprinkle with salt and pepper. Add half of beef to bacon drippings in Dutch oven and cook over high heat until well browned, using slotted spoon to transfer beef as it is browned to bowl with bacon. Repeat with remaining beef.

4   Reduce heat to medium-high. Add remaining 1 tablespoon oil to Dutch oven. Stir in flour until well blended and cook, stirring constantly, until flour browns. Gradually stir in broth and beer. Cook, stirring constantly, until sauce has thickened and boils.

5   Return beef mixture to Dutch oven; add thyme and bay leaf. Cover and place in oven. Bake until meat is tender, about 2 hours 30 minutes. Skim and discard fat from stew liquid; discard bay leaf.

EACH SERVING: ABOUT 370 CALORIES | 29G PROTEIN | 14G CARBOHYDRATE | 22G TOTAL FAT (7G SATURATED) | 93MG CHOLESTEROL | 574MG SODIUM

CHOUCROUTE GARNI

For sauerkraut lovers! Serve this hearty, homey dish with some boiled potatoes, a pot of good-quality mustard, and a loaf of crusty bread.

ACTIVE TIME: 20 MINUTES · TOTAL TIME: 1 HOUR 10 MINUTES
MAKES: 6 MAIN-DISH SERVINGS

---

4 SLICES BACON, CUT INTO 1-INCH PIECES

¼ CUP WATER

1 LARGE ONION (12 OUNCES), THINLY SLICED

2 MCINTOSH APPLES, EACH PEELED, CUT INTO QUARTERS, AND THINLY SLICED

2 BAGS (16 OUNCES EACH) SAUERKRAUT, RINSED

1½ CUPS FRUITY WHITE WINE, SUCH AS RIESLING

6 JUNIPER BERRIES, CRUSHED

1 BAY LEAF

6 SMOKED PORK CHOPS (EACH 4 OUNCES, ½ INCH THICK)

1 POUND KIELBASA (SMOKED POLISH SAUSAGE)

---

1 In nonreactive 5-quart Dutch oven, combine bacon and water; cook over medium-low heat until bacon is lightly crisped, about 4 minutes. Add onion and cook, stirring frequently, until onion is tender and golden, about 7 minutes.

2 Add apples and cook until tender, about 3 minutes. Stir in sauerkraut, wine, juniper berries, and bay leaf and heat to boiling. Reduce heat; cover and simmer 15 minutes.

3 Nestle pork chops and kielbasa into cabbage mixture; cover and cook until pork is heated through and sauerkraut is tender, about 20 minutes. Discard bay leaf and serve.

EACH SERVING: ABOUT 525 CALORIES | 27G PROTEIN | 19G CARBOHYDRATE | 37G TOTAL FAT (13G SATURATED) | 106MG CHOLESTEROL | 3,151MG SODIUM

PORK LOIN WITH APPLES, POTATOES, AND SAGE

This sage-infused roast pork loin is a comforting one-dish meal—easy to cook, a snap to clean up, but so pretty on the platter, your guests won't realize it was a cinch to make. For photo, see page 94.

ACTIVE TIME: 15 MINUTES · TOTAL TIME: 1 HOUR 5 MINUTES PLUS STANDING
MAKES: 8 MAIN-DISH SERVINGS

3	TABLESPOONS BUTTER OR MARGARINE, SOFTENED	1	BONELESS PORK LOIN ROAST (3 POUNDS), TRIMMED OF FAT
2	TABLESPOONS CHOPPED FRESH SAGE LEAVES	1½	POUNDS BABY RED POTATOES, CUT IN HALF
1	TEASPOON SALT	1	LARGE ONION (12 OUNCES), CHOPPED
¼	TEASPOON COARSELY GROUND BLACK PEPPER	1½	POUNDS GALA OR JONAGOLD APPLES, CORED AND CUT INTO 8 WEDGES

1   Preheat oven to 450°F. In small bowl, mix 1 tablespoon butter, 1 tablespoon chopped sage, ½ teaspoon salt, and pepper. With hands, rub mixture all over pork loin.

2   In 15½" by 10½" jelly-roll pan, melt remaining 2 tablespoons butter in oven. Add potatoes, onion, and remaining ½ teaspoon salt and 1 tablespoon chopped sage to pan with butter; toss to coat. Push potatoes and onion to edges of pan and set small roasting rack in center; place pork on rack. Roast 20 minutes.

3   Arrange apples around pork in pan, and continue roasting 30 to 40 minutes, or until meat thermometer inserted into thickest part of pork registers 145°F. (Internal temperature will rise 5°F to 10°F upon standing.)

4   Transfer pork to warm platter; let stand 15 minutes to set juices for easier slicing. With slotted spoon, transfer potatoes, onion, and apples to platter with pork. Pour pan drippings into small cup. Skim off and discard fat from drippings. Serve pork, sliced, with drippings.

EACH SERVING: ABOUT 475 CALORIES | 36G PROTEIN | 34G CARBOHYDRATE | 22G TOTAL FAT (7G SATURATED) | 102MG CHOLESTEROL | 435MG SODIUM

ROAST IT RIGHT

Whether you're roasting a pork loin or a whole bird, here are some tips to help you achieve perfect results.

• Preheat the oven fully, allowing 10 to 15 minutes for your oven to reach the desired temperature before putting the meat in.

• Hold the lid. A roasting pan with a lid steams the food being roasted rather than cooking it by dry heat. This can be good for poultry and tough cuts of meat but not for tender cuts like pork loin. Our recipes specify when you need to cover a roast with a lid; otherwise, don't use one.

• Roast in the center of the oven unless otherwise instructed. Roasting on the upper rack enhances browning on the top surfaces, while roasting on the lower rack increases browning on the bottom. If your roast needs additional browning on either the top or bottom, move the pan accordingly.

• Always use a meat thermometer—it's the only way to guarantee that the meat has been roasted to desired doneness. Be sure to insert the thermometer into the center or thickest part of the roast, and don't touch any bone or fatty sections, as that will give an inaccurate reading.

• Remove a roast from the oven when it is 5° to 10°F cooler than the desired temperature: The temperature will continue to rise as the meat stands. Letting the roast stand for about 10 minutes after cooking also allows time for the juices to redistribute evenly before carving and serving.

COUNTRY CAPTAIN CASSEROLE

Though the exact origin of this well-known dish is often debated, its great flavor is never in dispute.

ACTIVE TIME: 30 MINUTES · TOTAL TIME: 1 HOUR 30 MINUTES
MAKES: 8 MAIN-DISH SERVINGS

---

2   TABLESPOONS PLUS 1 TEASPOON VEGETABLE OIL

2   CHICKENS (3½ POUNDS EACH), EACH CUT INTO 8 PIECES AND SKIN REMOVED FROM ALL BUT WINGS

2   MEDIUM ONIONS, CHOPPED

1   LARGE GRANNY SMITH APPLE, PEELED, CORED, AND CHOPPED

1   LARGE GREEN PEPPER, CHOPPED

3   LARGE GARLIC CLOVES, FINELY CHOPPED

1   TABLESPOON GRATED, PEELED FRESH GINGER

3   TABLESPOONS CURRY POWDER

½   TEASPOON COARSELY GROUND BLACK PEPPER

¼   TEASPOON GROUND CUMIN

1   CAN (28 OUNCES) PLUM TOMATOES IN PUREE

1   CAN (14½ OUNCES) CHICKEN BROTH

½   CUP DARK SEEDLESS RAISINS

1   TEASPOON SALT

¼   CUP CHOPPED FRESH PARSLEY

---

1   In nonreactive 8-quart Dutch oven, heat 2 tablespoons oil over medium-high heat until very hot. Add chicken, in batches, and cook until golden brown, about 5 minutes per side. With slotted spoon, transfer chicken pieces to bowl as they are browned.

2   Preheat oven to 350°F. In same Dutch oven, heat remaining 1 teaspoon oil over medium-high heat. Add onions, apple, green pepper, garlic, and ginger; cook, stirring frequently, 2 minutes. Reduce heat to medium; cover and cook 5 minutes longer.

3   Stir in curry powder, black pepper, and cumin; cook 1 minute. Add tomatoes with their puree, broth, raisins, salt, and chicken pieces. Heat to boiling over high heat; boil 1 minute. Cover and place in oven. Bake 1 hour, until instant-read thermometer inserted into thickest part of chicken registers 165°F. Sprinkle with parsley.

EACH SERVING: ABOUT 345 CALORIES | 43G PROTEIN | 19G CARBOHYDRATE | 11G TOTAL FAT (2G SATURATED) | 133MG CHOLESTEROL | 825MG SODIUM ☺ 🍲

ROASTED CHICKEN WITH WINTER VEGETABLES

This hearty meal is foolproof and hassle-free.

ACTIVE TIME: 15 MINUTES · TOTAL TIME: 1 HOUR
MAKES: 4 MAIN-DISH SERVINGS

1 LARGE ONION (10 TO 12 OUNCES), CUT INTO ½-INCH-THICK SLICES

1 POUND BABY RED POTATOES, EACH CUT IN HALF OR QUARTERS IF LARGE

4 LARGE CARROTS (1 POUND TOTAL), EACH CUT INTO 2-INCH-LONG PIECES

2 SMALL TURNIPS (2 OUNCES EACH), PEELED AND EACH CUT INTO 6 WEDGES

1 SMALL FENNEL BULB (6 OUNCES), TRIMMED, CORED, AND CUT INTO 6 WEDGES

8 SPRIGS FRESH THYME, PLUS ADDITIONAL FOR GARNISH

7 GARLIC CLOVES, CRUSHED WITH SIDE OF CHEF'S KNIFE

1 TABLESPOON PLUS 1 TEASPOON OLIVE OIL

⅝ TEASPOON SALT

⅝ TEASPOON GROUND BLACK PEPPER

1 WHOLE CHICKEN (3 TO 3½ POUNDS)

1 Preheat oven to 450°F. In 18" by 12" jelly-roll pan, arrange onion slices in single layer in center. In large bowl, toss potatoes, carrots, turnips, fennel, 4 thyme sprigs, 3 garlic cloves, 1 tablespoon oil, and ¼ teaspoon each salt and pepper until well mixed. Spread in even layer around onion slices in pan.

2 If necessary, remove bag with giblets and neck from chicken cavity; discard or reserve for another use. Rub chicken cavity with ¼ teaspoon each salt and pepper. Place remaining 4 thyme sprigs and 4 garlic cloves in cavity and tie legs together with kitchen string. Rub remaining 1 teaspoon oil on chicken and sprinkle with remaining ⅛ teaspoon each salt and pepper.

3 Place chicken, breast side up, on onion slices in pan. Roast 45 minutes or until meat thermometer inserted into thickest part of thigh reaches 165°F. Let chicken stand on pan 10 minutes to set juices for easier carving. Meanwhile, transfer vegetables around chicken to serving platter, leaving space in center for chicken.

4 Transfer chicken and onion to serving platter with vegetables, tilting chicken slightly as you lift to allow any juices inside to run into pan. Skim and discard fat from juices in pan; pour into small bowl and serve with chicken. Garnish with additional thyme sprigs.

EACH SERVING: ABOUT 555 CALORIES | 45G PROTEIN | 37G CARBOHYDRATE | 25G TOTAL FAT (6G SATURATED) | 160MG CHOLESTEROL | 405MG SODIUM

INDIAN CHICKEN AND RICE CASSEROLE

Traditionally made with lamb, our lighter take substitutes skinless chicken breasts. For tasty garnishes, see "Condiments for Curry," opposite.

ACTIVE TIME: 30 MINUTES · TOTAL TIME: 1 HOUR 5 MINUTES
MAKES: 6 MAIN-DISH SERVINGS

1 CAN (14½ OUNCES) CHICKEN BROTH

1 CUP BASMATI RICE

3 GARLIC CLOVES, PEELED

1 PIECE (1" BY ½") FRESH GINGER, PEELED AND COARSELY CHOPPED

¼ CUP SWEETENED FLAKED COCONUT

1 LARGE ONION (10 TO 12 OUNCES), HALVED AND THINLY SLICED

3 TEASPOONS VEGETABLE OIL

1 SMALL RED PEPPER, CUT INTO ½-INCH PIECES

1 POUND SKINLESS, BONELESS CHICKEN BREAST HALVES, CUT INTO ½-INCH PIECES

¾ TEASPOON GROUND CUMIN

¾ TEASPOON GROUND CORIANDER

½ TEASPOON SALT

⅛ TEASPOON CAYENNE (GROUND RED) PEPPER

2 CUPS CAULIFLOWER FLORETS (FROM ½ MEDIUM HEAD), CUT INTO ½-INCH PIECES

¾ CUP WATER

1 PACKAGE (10 OUNCES) FROZEN PEAS AND CARROTS

1 CAN (14½ OUNCES) DICED TOMATOES

1 CONTAINER (8 OUNCES) PLAIN NONFAT YOGURT

1   Preheat oven to 350°F. In 2-cup measuring cup, add enough *water* to chicken broth to equal 2 cups. In 2-quart saucepan, heat chicken broth mixture to boiling over high. Place rice in shallow 2½-quart casserole; stir in boiling broth mixture. Cover casserole tightly and bake 20 minutes or until rice is tender and liquid is absorbed. Remove casserole from oven; set aside.

2   Meanwhile, in food processor with knife blade attached, or in blender on medium speed, blend garlic, ginger, coconut, and half of onion slices until a paste forms; set aside.

3   In nonstick 12-inch skillet, heat 2 teaspoons vegetable oil over medium heat. Add red pepper and remaining onion slices and cook until golden, about 10 minutes. With slotted spoon, transfer vegetables to large bowl.

4   Add garlic mixture to same skillet and cook 8 to 10 minutes or until golden. Add chicken pieces and remaining 1 teaspoon oil and cook, stirring occasionally, until chicken is lightly browned on the outside and loses its pink color on the inside. Add cumin, coriander, salt, and cayenne and cook 2 minutes longer. Transfer chicken mixture to bowl with vegetables.

CONDIMENTS FOR CURRY

Present each condiment in a small bowl, with a serving spoon if needed, so everyone can choose their favorites. Or simply sprinkle two or three items on top of each serving of curry before serving.

Dried Fruit
Golden or black raisins
Dried apricots
Dried cherries
Shredded unsweetened coconut

Herbs and Vegetables
Fresh cilantro or parsley
Cucumber sticks
Diced fresh tomatoes

Nuts (all may be toasted)
Slivered almonds
Pistachios
Chopped peanuts

Sauces and Pickles
Plain yogurt or raita
Mango or mint chutney
Indian pickles, such as lime or mango pickles

5   To same skillet, add cauliflower and water; heat to boiling over medium-high. Reduce heat to low; cover and simmer 6 minutes. Add frozen peas and carrots, and tomatoes with their juice; heat to boiling over medium-high. Reduce heat to low; uncover and cook 2 minutes longer or until cauliflower is tender and peas and carrots are heated through. Transfer cauliflower mixture to bowl with chicken. Stir in yogurt until well mixed.

6   With fork, fluff rice. Top cooked rice with chicken mixture. Bake, uncovered, 15 minutes longer or until heated through. Serve with a selection of the garnishes described in box above.

EACH SERVING: ABOUT 335 CALORIES | 28G PROTEIN | 45G CARBOHYDRATE | 6G TOTAL FAT (2G SATURATED) | 45MG CHOLESTEROL | 760MG SODIUM ☺ 🍴

ROASTED BROCCOLI AND CHICKEN BAKE

Nutty barley, skinless chicken breast, and heaps of bright green broccoli florets make this tasty casserole as wholesome as it is delicious.

ACTIVE TIME: 25 MINUTES · TOTAL TIME: 50 MINUTES
MAKES: 4 MAIN-DISH SERVINGS

---

1 CUP PEARL BARLEY	1 LARGE CARROT, PEELED AND FINELY CHOPPED
3 CUPS REDUCED-SODIUM CHICKEN BROTH	1 SMALL ONION, FINELY CHOPPED
2 TABLESPOONS OLIVE OIL	2 TEASPOONS FRESH THYME LEAVES, CHOPPED
1 POUND SKINLESS, BONELESS CHICKEN BREAST HALVES, CUT INTO 1-INCH CHUNKS	2 GARLIC CLOVES, FINELY CHOPPED
	8 OUNCES MUSHROOMS, THINLY SLICED
⅜ TEASPOON SALT	¼ CUP WATER
¼ TEASPOON GROUND BLACK PEPPER	6 CUPS SMALL BROCCOLI FLORETS (SEE TIP)

1   Preheat oven to 400°F.

2   In large microwave-safe bowl, stir together barley and broth. Cover with vented plastic wrap; microwave on High 20 to 25 minutes or until most of liquid is absorbed, stirring once.

3   Meanwhile, in 12-inch skillet, heat 1 tablespoon oil over medium-high heat. Add chicken; sprinkle with ¼ teaspoon salt and pepper. Cook 4 minutes or until golden, stirring once. With slotted spoon, transfer chicken to medium bowl.

4   To skillet, add carrot, onion, and thyme; cook 3 minutes, stirring. Add garlic; cook 30 seconds, stirring, then add mushrooms and water, scraping up browned bits. Cook 2 minutes; remove from heat. Stir in chicken and barley; transfer to shallow 3-quart baking dish.

5   Toss broccoli with remaining ⅛ teaspoon salt and remaining 1 tablespoon oil; arrange on top of barley mixture. Bake 20 to 25 minutes or until broccoli is tender.

TIP   While it's easy to buy precut broccoli florets, we like to cut them from the heads (about two in this case) and save the stems for another meal.

EACH SERVING: ABOUT 430 CALORIES | 35G PROTEIN | 51G CARBOHYDRATE | 11G TOTAL FAT (2G SATURATED) | 73MG CHOLESTEROL | 735MG SODIUM ☺

CHICKEN SHEPHERD'S PIE

Shepherd's pie was originally created as a way to utilize Sunday's leftovers. We've lightened the filling and topped it off with a mantle of creamy, chive-flecked mashed potatoes.

ACTIVE TIME: 45 MINUTES · TOTAL TIME: 1 HOUR 5 MINUTES
MAKES: 6 MAIN-DISH SERVINGS

2 POUNDS ALL-PURPOSE POTATOES (6 MEDIUM), PEELED AND CUT INTO 1-INCH PIECES

2 TABLESPOONS VEGETABLE OIL

2 CARROTS, PEELED AND FINELY CHOPPED

1 LARGE ONION (12 OUNCES), FINELY CHOPPED

1 LARGE RED PEPPER, FINELY CHOPPED

2 TABLESPOONS BUTTER OR MARGARINE

1 TEASPOON SALT

¾ CUP MILK

2 TABLESPOONS CHOPPED FRESH CHIVES OR GREEN-ONION TOPS

10 OUNCES MUSHROOMS, TRIMMED AND THICKLY SLICED

1¼ CUPS CHICKEN BROTH

1 TABLESPOON ALL-PURPOSE FLOUR

1½ POUNDS GROUND CHICKEN

¼ TEASPOON COARSELY GROUND BLACK PEPPER

¼ TEASPOON DRIED THYME

2 TABLESPOONS KETCHUP

1 TABLESPOON WORCESTERSHIRE SAUCE

1 In 3-quart saucepan, combine potatoes and enough *water* to cover; heat to boiling over high heat. Reduce heat; cover and simmer until potatoes are tender, about 15 minutes.

2 Meanwhile, in 12-inch skillet, heat 1 tablespoon oil over medium-high heat. Add carrots and cook 5 minutes. Add onion and red pepper and cook, stirring occasionally, until vegetables are tender and lightly browned, about 10 minutes longer. With slotted spoon, transfer vegetables to bowl.

3 When potatoes are tender, drain. Mash potatoes in saucepan with butter and ½ teaspoon salt. Gradually add milk; mash until mixture is smooth and well blended. Stir in chives; set aside.

4 In same skillet, heat remaining 1 tablespoon oil over medium-high heat. Add mushrooms and cook until well browned, about 10 minutes. Transfer to bowl with vegetables.

5 In 2-cup measuring cup, blend broth and flour until smooth; set aside.

6 Preheat oven to 400°F. In same skillet, cook ground chicken, black pepper, thyme, and remaining ½ teaspoon salt over high heat, stirring occasionally, until chicken is lightly browned and any liquid in skillet has evaporated, 7 to 10 minutes. Stir in ketchup, Worcestershire, cooked vegetables, and broth

mixture. Cook, stirring constantly, until liquid has thickened and boils, 3 to 5 minutes.

7   Spoon mixture into a shallow 2-quart casserole; top with mashed potatoes. Place casserole on foil-lined baking sheet to catch any overflow during baking. Bake until the potato topping is lightly browned, 20 to 25 minutes.

EACH SERVING: ABOUT 415 CALORIES | 26G PROTEIN | 33G CARBOHYDRATE | 20G TOTAL FAT (6G SATURATED) | 109MG CHOLESTEROL | 848MG SODIUM 😊 🍲

MUSTARD-DILL SALMON WITH POTATOES

This elegant dish is surprisingly simple to make. While the potatoes cook, you can broil the salmon and whip up the no-cook sauce.

ACTIVE TIME: 20 MINUTES · TOTAL TIME: 30 MINUTES
MAKES: 4 MAIN-DISH SERVINGS

12 OUNCES SMALL RED POTATOES, CUT INTO 1-INCH CHUNKS

12 OUNCES SMALL WHITE POTATOES, CUT INTO 1-INCH CHUNKS

1½ TEASPOONS SALT

3 TABLESPOONS CHOPPED FRESH DILL

½ TEASPOON COARSELY GROUND BLACK PEPPER

4 PIECES SALMON FILLET (6 OUNCES EACH)

2 TABLESPOONS LIGHT MAYONNAISE

1 TABLESPOON WHITE WINE VINEGAR

2 TEASPOONS DIJON MUSTARD

¾ TEASPOON SUGAR

1 In 3-quart saucepan, place potatoes, 1 teaspoon salt, and enough *water* to cover; heat to boiling over high heat. Reduce heat to low; cover and simmer 15 minutes or until potatoes are fork-tender. Drain potatoes and toss with 1 tablespoon dill, ¼ teaspoon salt, and ¼ teaspoon pepper; keep potatoes warm.

2 Meanwhile, preheat broiler. Grease rack in broiling pan. Place salmon on rack; sprinkle with ⅛ teaspoon each salt and pepper. Broil salmon at closest position to source of heat 8 to 10 minutes, until fish flakes easily and instant-read thermometer inserted horizontally into fillet registers 145°F.

3 While salmon is broiling, prepare sauce: In small bowl, mix mayonnaise, vinegar, mustard, and sugar with remaining 2 tablespoons dill, ⅛ teaspoon salt, and ⅛ teaspoon pepper.

4 Serve salmon with sauce and potatoes.

EACH SERVING: ABOUT 335 CALORIES | 37G PROTEIN | 31G CARBOHYDRATE | 7G TOTAL FAT (1G SATURATED) | 86MG CHOLESTEROL | 655MG SODIUM ♥ ☺

SHRIMP CREOLE

This spicy one-dish meal is a New Orleans classic. The rice bakes right in the pan along with peppers, okra, chorizo, shrimp, and tomatoes.

ACTIVE TIME: 45 MINUTES · TOTAL TIME: 1 HOUR 15 MINUTES
MAKES: 6 MAIN-DISH SERVINGS

1 TABLESPOON OLIVE OIL	2 CLOVES GARLIC, MINCED
1 LARGE ONION (10 TO 12 OUNCES), CUT INTO ½-INCH PIECES	1½ CUPS RICE, PARBOILED
1 MEDIUM GREEN PEPPER, COARSELY CHOPPED	1 CAN (14½ OUNCES) STEWED TOMATOES
1 MEDIUM RED PEPPER, COARSELY CHOPPED	1 BOTTLE (8 OUNCES) CLAM JUICE
8 OUNCES READY-TO-EAT CHORIZO SAUSAGE OR PEPPERONI, CUT INTO ¼-INCH-THICK SLICES	1 PACKAGE (10 OUNCES) FROZEN WHOLE OKRA, THAWED
	1 POUND MEDIUM SHRIMP, SHELLED AND DEVEINED

1 Preheat oven to 350°F. In 3- to 3½-quart Dutch oven, heat oil over medium heat until hot. Add onion and peppers and cook about 10 minutes, stirring frequently, until tender and lightly browned. Add sliced chorizo and garlic and cook 5 minutes longer until chorizo is lightly browned.

2 Stir in rice, stewed tomatoes, clam juice, and 1¼ *cups water*; over high heat, heat to boiling. Cover Dutch oven; place in oven and bake 20 minutes.

3 Stir okra and shrimp into rice mixture; cover and bake 10 minutes longer or until rice and shrimp are tender.

EACH SERVING: ABOUT 405 CALORIES | 26G PROTEIN | 34G CARBOHYDRATE | 18G TOTAL FAT (6G SATURATED) | 127MG CHOLESTEROL | 800MG SODIUM ☺

LAYERED THREE-BEAN CASSEROLE

This Mexican-inspired vegetarian casserole layers three kinds of beans with tortillas, cheese, and salsa. You can assemble it up to a day in advance. If you're using home-cooked beans, see "Better Beans" on page 39 for preparation tips.

ACTIVE TIME: 20 MINUTES · TOTAL TIME: 1 HOUR 30 MINUTES
MAKES: 6 MAIN-DISH SERVINGS

---

3   POBLANO PEPPERS

1   CUP REDUCED-FAT SOUR CREAM

¼   CUP LOW-FAT (1%) MILK

9   CORN TORTILLAS (4-INCH DIAMETER)

2   CUPS SALSA VERDE

1½ CUPS COOKED BLACK BEANS, OR
    1 CAN (15 OUNCES) LOW-SODIUM
    BLACK BEANS

6   OUNCES MONTEREY JACK CHEESE,
    SHREDDED (1½ CUPS)

1   CAN (16 OUNCES) REFRIED BEANS

1½ CUPS COOKED PINK BEANS, OR
    1 CAN (15 OUNCES) LOW-SODIUM
    PINK BEANS

¼   SMALL RED ONION, VERY THINLY SLICED

½   CUP FRESH CILANTRO LEAVES, CHOPPED

1   Arrange oven rack 5 inches from heat source. Preheat broiler. In broiling pan lined with foil, arrange poblano peppers in single layer. Broil 10 to 15 minutes or until blackened all over, turning occasionally to evenly blacken. Wrap peppers in foil; let cool. Reset oven control to 350°F. Remove peppers from foil; peel off skin and discard. Remove and discard stems and seeds; thinly slice peppers.

2   In medium bowl, combine sour cream and milk until well blended. In 9-inch square baking dish, arrange 3 tortillas in single layer, tearing 1 tortilla in half to fit. Top with one-third each of the salsa and the sour cream mixture, all of the black beans, one-third of the cheese, and one-third of the sliced poblano peppers, in that order, spreading each in an even layer. Repeat layering two more times, with refried beans in center layer and pink beans on top. (Can be prepared to this point up to 1 day ahead; cover and refrigerate, adding 10 minutes to bake time.) Place baking dish on jelly-roll pan to catch any drips and bake uncovered 40 to 55 minutes or until mixture bubbles and top browns.

3   Cool in dish on wire rack 10 minutes. Sprinkle with onion slices and cilantro to serve.

EACH SERVING: ABOUT 490 CALORIES | 24G PROTEIN | 65G CARBOHYDRATE | 16G TOTAL FAT (9G SATURATED) | 47MG CHOLESTEROL | 890MG SODIUM

VEGGIE ENCHILADAS

Fresh cilantro gives this hearty casserole real southwestern flavor.

ACTIVE TIME: 25 MINUTES · TOTAL TIME: 45 MINUTES
MAKES: 6 MAIN-DISH SERVINGS

2   TEASPOONS OLIVE OIL

1   SMALL ZUCCHINI (8 OUNCES), CUT INTO ½-INCH PIECES

1   MEDIUM ONION, CHOPPED

1   MEDIUM RED PEPPER, CHOPPED

2   CANS (15 TO 19 OUNCES EACH) NO-SALT-ADDED WHITE KIDNEY BEANS (CANNELLINI), RINSED AND DRAINED

½   CUP VEGETABLE OR CHICKEN BROTH

2   GARLIC CLOVES, MINCED

1   CAN (15¼ OUNCES) NO-SALT-ADDED WHOLE-KERNEL CORN, DRAINED

2   PICKLED JALAPEÑO CHILES, MINCED, WITH SEEDS

1   CUP LOOSELY PACKED CHOPPED FRESH CILANTRO LEAVES AND STEMS

6   FLOUR TORTILLAS (8-INCH DIAMETER)

1   JAR (15½ OUNCES) MILD SALSA

⅓   CUP SHREDDED MONTEREY JACK CHEESE

LIME WEDGES FOR GARNISH

1   In nonstick 12-inch skillet, heat oil over medium heat. Add zucchini, onion, and red pepper; cook until vegetables are tender and golden, 10 to 15 minutes, stirring frequently.

2   Meanwhile, in food processor with knife blade attached, or in blender at medium speed, blend half of beans with broth until almost smooth. Transfer bean mixture to large bowl; stir in remaining beans and set aside.

3   To vegetables in skillet, add garlic and cook 1 minute longer. Stir in corn and jalapeños; cook 2 minutes longer. Transfer vegetable mixture to bowl with beans; stir in cilantro until mixed.

4   Preheat oven to 375°F. Spoon about ¾ cup bean mixture along center of each tortilla. Fold sides of tortilla over filling, overlapping them slightly.

5   Spoon ½ cup salsa into bottom of 13" by 9" glass or ceramic baking dish. Place enchiladas, seam side down, on top of salsa. Spoon remaining salsa over enchiladas; sprinkle with cheese. Bake 20 minutes, until cheese is bubbly and enchiladas are hot throughout. Serve with lime wedges.

EACH SERVING: ABOUT 415 CALORIES | 17G PROTEIN | 70G CARBOHYDRATE | 8G TOTAL FAT (2G SATURATED) | 6MG CHOLESTEROL | 700MG SODIUM ☺ 🍲

SPINACH AND FETA BREAD PUDDING

If you love the comfort of warm, sweet bread pudding for dessert, treat yourself to this savory version for brunch or supper.

ACTIVE TIME: 15 MINUTES · TOTAL TIME: 40 MINUTES PLUS STANDING
MAKES: 6 MAIN-DISH SERVINGS

2   TABLESPOONS BUTTER OR MARGARINE

1   MEDIUM ONION, CHOPPED

6   LARGE EGGS

2   CUPS LOW-FAT (1%) MILK

3   TABLESPOONS CHOPPED FRESH DILL

½   TEASPOON FRESHLY GRATED LEMON PEEL

½   TEASPOON SALT

½   TEASPOON COARSELY GROUND BLACK PEPPER

1   PACKAGE (10 OUNCES) FROZEN CHOPPED SPINACH, THAWED AND SQUEEZED DRY

4   OUNCES FETA CHEESE, CUT INTO ½-INCH CUBES

8   SLICES FIRM WHITE BREAD, CUT INTO ¾-INCH PIECES

1   Preheat oven to 350°F. In nonstick 12-inch skillet with oven-safe handle, melt butter over medium heat. Add onion and cook until tender, about 10 minutes.

2   In medium bowl, with wire whisk or fork, beat eggs, milk, dill, lemon peel, salt, and pepper until blended. With rubber spatula, stir in onion, spinach, and cheese. Gently stir in bread pieces. Pour mixture into skillet; let stand 15 minutes to allow bread to absorb liquid.

3   Cook mixture over medium heat 4 minutes, without stirring, or until mixture begins to set around edge. Place skillet in oven; bake 20 to 25 minutes, until knife inserted in center of bread pudding comes out clean.

4   Remove bread pudding from oven; let stand 5 minutes before serving. To serve, cut into wedges.

EACH SERVING: ABOUT 295 CALORIES | 16G PROTEIN | 25G CARBOHYDRATE | 15G TOTAL FAT (6G SATURATED) | 233MG CHOLESTEROL | 655MG SODIUM ☺

OVEN-BAKED DRUMSTICKS AND DIPPING VEGGIES

Dipping food is fun for kids and adults alike. For photo, see page 2.

ACTIVE TIME: 35 MINUTES · TOTAL TIME: 55 MINUTES
MAKES: 6 MAIN-DISH SERVINGS

3   TABLESPOONS DIJON MUSTARD

3   TABLESPOONS LIGHT MAYONNAISE

12 LARGE CHICKEN DRUMSTICKS
    (3½ POUNDS), SKIN REMOVED

1   LEMON

1   CUP PANKO (JAPANESE-STYLE
    BREAD CRUMBS)

½   CUP FINELY GRATED PARMESAN CHEESE

2   TABLESPOONS OLIVE OIL

⅛   TEASPOON CAYENNE (GROUND RED)
    PEPPER

⅞   TEASPOON SALT

⅜   TEASPOON GROUND BLACK PEPPER

⅓   CUP PLAIN NONFAT YOGURT

¼   CUP PACKED FRESH BASIL LEAVES,
    FINELY CHOPPED

1   POUND ASPARAGUS

CARROTS, CELERY STICKS, GREEN BEANS,
AND SLICED PEPPERS, FOR SERVING

1   Arrange oven rack in top third of oven. Preheat oven to 450°F. Line 18" by 12" jelly-roll pan with foil.

2   In large bowl, stir mustard and mayonnaise until well combined; add chicken pieces and toss until evenly coated. Set aside.

3   From lemon, grate 1 teaspoon peel into 9-inch pie plate and squeeze 1 tablespoon juice into small bowl. In pie plate with lemon peel, combine panko, grated Parmesan, oil, cayenne, ⅛ teaspoon salt, and ⅛ teaspoon pepper. Dredge 1 drumstick in crumb mixture until well coated, shake off excess, and place on prepared pan. Repeat with remaining chicken and crumb mixture. Bake 30 minutes or until crust is golden brown and juices run clear when chicken is pierced with tip of knife.

3   Meanwhile, in small bowl with lemon juice, stir yogurt, ¼ teaspoon salt, and remaining ¼ teaspoon pepper until smooth. Stir in basil.

4   Fill 12-inch skillet with 1 inch water. Cover and heat to boiling on high. Add asparagus and remaining ½ teaspoon salt. Cook, uncovered, 4 to 5 minutes or until bright green and crisp-tender, turning occasionally for even cooking. Rinse under cold running water; drain.

5   Serve chicken with asparagus and assorted raw vegetables, along with dipping sauce on the side.

EACH SERVING: ABOUT 335 CALORIES | 37G PROTEIN | 11G CARBOHYDRATE | 15G TOTAL FAT (4G SATURATED) | 122MG CHOLESTEROL | 560MG SODIUM ☺ ▦

CABBAGE AND BULGUR CASSEROLE

We layered Napa cabbage with a filling that's healthy and tastes great.

ACTIVE TIME: 45 MINUTES · TOTAL TIME: 1 HOUR 25 MINUTES
MAKES: 6 MAIN-DISH SERVINGS

2 CUPS WATER	3 GREEN ONIONS, SLICED
1½ CUPS BULGUR	2 TABLESPOONS MINCED, PEELED FRESH GINGER
1 TABLESPOON VEGETABLE OIL	2 TABLESPOONS PLUS 1 TEASPOON SOY SAUCE
2 CARROTS, PEELED AND DICED	
2 STALKS CELERY, DICED	2 TABLESPOONS SEASONED RICE VINEGAR
1 RED BELL PEPPER, DICED	1 CAN (14½ OUNCES) DICED TOMATOES
½ SMALL HEAD NAPA CABBAGE (CHINESE CABBAGE), CORED AND CUT CROSSWISE INTO 2-INCH PIECES TO EQUAL ABOUT 12 CUPS LEAFY TOPS AND 2 CUPS CRUNCHY STEMS	2 TABLESPOONS BROWN SUGAR
	2 TABLESPOONS CHOPPED FRESH PARSLEY FOR GARNISH
3 GARLIC CLOVES, CRUSHED WITH GARLIC PRESS	

1 Preheat oven to 350°F.

2 In 2-quart saucepan, heat 1½ cups water to boiling over high heat; stir in bulgur. Remove saucepan from heat; cover and set aside.

3 In 5-quart Dutch oven, heat oil over medium-high heat. Add carrots, celery, and red pepper; cook 5 minutes. Add cabbage stems and cook until vegetables are tender, 7 minutes longer. Reduce heat to low; add garlic, green onions, and ginger and cook 1 minute longer, stirring.

4 Add remaining ½ cup water; heat to boiling over high heat. Reduce heat to low; simmer 1 minute, stirring. Remove Dutch oven from heat; stir in 2 tablespoons soy sauce, 1 tablespoon vinegar, and cooked bulgur.

5 In small bowl, combine tomatoes with their juice, brown sugar, and remaining 1 teaspoon soy sauce and 1 tablespoon vinegar.

6 In 3-quart casserole, place half of cabbage leaves; top with bulgur mixture, then remaining cabbage leaves. Spoon tomato mixture over top. Cover casserole and bake until hot in center and top layer of cabbage leaves is wilted, about 40 minutes. Sprinkle with parsley before serving.

EACH SERVING: ABOUT 220 CALORIES | 7G PROTEIN | 43G CARBOHYDRATE | 3G TOTAL FAT (0G SATURATED) | 0MG CHOLESTEROL | 800MG SODIUM ☺ 🍲

SALADS & SANDWICHES

Whether you're looking for a quick lunch or a light dinner, a big bowl of salad or a stuffed sandwich are easy options. Toss together our chicken and raspberry, shrimp and tomato, or classic Niçoise salads in minutes. Or serve chicken or steak in a lettuce wrap. Love a hearty sandwich? Sink your teeth into Philly Cheese Steaks or slow-cooked pulled pork. Or pack up a Smoked Turkey and Mango Wrap or Chicken Caesar Pocket for the road.

KEY TO ICONS

⊘ 30 minutes or less　♥ Heart healthy　☺ Low calorie　▤ Make ahead　⌂ Slow cooker

Turkey and Spicy Hummus Clubs (page 142)

NIÇOISE SALAD

As the story goes, the first Niçoise salad was created in eighteenth-century France, and it's been a hit ever since.

ACTIVE TIME: 35 MINUTES · TOTAL TIME: 1 HOUR

MAKES: 4 MAIN-DISH SERVINGS

1 TABLESPOON WHITE WINE VINEGAR	8 OUNCES FRENCH GREEN BEANS (HARICOTS VERTS) OR REGULAR GREEN BEANS, TRIMMED (SEE TIP)
1 TABLESPOON FRESH LEMON JUICE	
1 TABLESPOON MINCED SHALLOT	
1 TEASPOON DIJON MUSTARD	1 HEAD BOSTON LETTUCE, LEAVES SEPARATED
1 TEASPOON ANCHOVY PASTE	
¼ TEASPOON SUGAR	12 CHERRY TOMATOES, EACH CUT IN HALF
¼ TEASPOON COARSELY GROUND BLACK PEPPER	1 CAN (12 OUNCES) SOLID WHITE TUNA PACKED IN WATER, DRAINED AND FLAKED
3 TABLESPOONS EXTRA-VIRGIN OLIVE OIL	
1 POUND MEDIUM RED POTATOES, NOT PEELED, CUT INTO ¼-INCH-THICK SLICES	2 LARGE HARD-COOKED EGGS, PEELED AND EACH CUT INTO QUARTERS
	½ CUP NIÇOISE OLIVES

1 Prepare dressing: In small bowl, with wire whisk, mix vinegar, lemon juice, shallot, mustard, anchovy paste, sugar, and pepper until blended. In thin, steady stream, whisk in oil until blended.

2 In 3-quart saucepan, combine potatoes and enough *water* to cover; heat to boiling over high heat. Reduce heat; cover and simmer until tender, about 10 minutes. Drain.

3 Meanwhile, in 10-inch skillet, heat 1 *inch water* to boiling over high heat. Add green beans; heat to boiling. Reduce heat to low and cook until tender-crisp, 6 to 8 minutes. Drain; rinse with cold running water. Drain.

4 To serve, pour half of dressing into medium bowl. Add lettuce leaves and toss to coat. Line large platter with dressed lettuce leaves. Arrange potatoes, green beans, cherry tomatoes, tuna, hard-cooked eggs, and olives in separate piles on lettuce. Drizzle remaining dressing over salad.

TIP *Haricots verts* are very thin, delicately flavored green beans. Look for fresh crisp beans with a bright color.

EACH SERVING: ABOUT 440 CALORIES | 30G PROTEIN | 30G CARBOHYDRATE | 23G TOTAL FAT (4G SATURATED) | 140MG CHOLESTEROL | 716MG SODIUM ☺

BEST TUNA SALAD

You can enjoy this simple family favorite two ways—on a sandwich or on a bed of salad greens. For a change of pace, try the tasty variations.

TOTAL TIME: 10 MINUTES

MAKES: 1¼ CUPS OR 2 MAIN-DISH SERVINGS

1   CAN (6 OUNCES) CHUNK LIGHT TUNA PACKED IN WATER, DRAINED

¼   CUP FINELY CHOPPED CELERY

3   TABLESPOONS LIGHT MAYONNAISE

2   TEASPOONS FRESH LEMON JUICE

BAGUETTE OR OTHER FAVORITE BREAD (OPTIONAL)

In small bowl, with fork, combine all ingredients except baguette. Cover and refrigerate if not serving right away. Serve on baguette if you like.

EACH SERVING WITHOUT BREAD: ABOUT 170 CALORIES | 19G PROTEIN | 1G CARBOHYDRATE 11G TOTAL FAT (3G SATURATED) | 30MG CHOLESTEROL | 415MG SODIUM

CURRIED TUNA

Prepare Best Tuna Salad as above. Stir in **½ cup finely chopped Granny Smith apple** and **1 teaspoon curry powder**. Serve on **raisin-walnut or sourdough bread** if you like.

EACH SERVING WITHOUT BREAD: ABOUT 190 CALORIES | 20G PROTEIN | 7G CARBOHYDRATE 11G TOTAL FAT (3G SATURATED) | 30MG CHOLESTEROL | 415MG SODIUM

SOUTHWESTERN TUNA

Prepare Best Tuna Salad as above. Stir in **2 tablespoons chopped fresh cilantro leaves** and **1 pickled jalapeño chile**, finely chopped. Serve rolled up in **warm flour tortillas** if you like.

EACH SERVING WITHOUT TORTILLA: ABOUT 170 CALORIES | 19G PROTEIN | 2G CARBOHYDRATE | 11G TOTAL FAT (3G SATURATED) | 30MG CHOLESTEROL | 510MG SODIUM

SHRIMP AND TOMATO SUMMER SALAD

This Greek-inspired salad is best in summer when tomatoes are at their peak and fresh herbs are plentiful. In the off-seasons, grape tomatoes, cut in half, are a good substitute.

TOTAL TIME: 25 MINUTES

MAKES: 6 MAIN-DISH SERVINGS

2 TABLESPOONS OLIVE OIL

2 TABLESPOONS RED WINE VINEGAR

¾ TEASPOON SALT

¼ TEASPOON COARSELY GROUND BLACK PEPPER

½ CUP LOOSELY PACKED FRESH PARSLEY LEAVES, CHOPPED

¼ CUP LOOSELY PACKED FRESH MINT LEAVES, THINLY SLICED

1 POUND SHELLED AND DEVEINED COOKED SHRIMP

4 RIPE LARGE TOMATOES (2½ POUNDS), CUT INTO 1-INCH CHUNKS

1 ENGLISH (SEEDLESS) CUCUMBER OR 4 KIRBY CUCUMBERS, CUT LENGTHWISE INTO QUARTERS, THEN CROSSWISE INTO 1-INCH CHUNKS

1 SMALL RED ONION, DICED

½ CUP CRUMBLED FETA CHEESE (2 OUNCES)

1   In serving bowl, whisk together oil, vinegar, salt, and pepper; stir in parsley and mint.

2   Add shrimp, tomatoes, cucumber, and onion to dressing in bowl; stir to combine. Sprinkle salad with feta to serve. Serve at room temperature or cover and refrigerate to serve later.

EACH SERVING: ABOUT 200 CALORIES | 20G PROTEIN | 13G CARBOHYDRATE | 8G TOTAL FAT (2G SATURATED) | 156MG CHOLESTEROL | 585MG SODIUM ♥ ☺ 🍴

CHICKEN AND RASPBERRY SALAD

This satisfying, healthful salad features grilled avocado slices, a buttery counterpart to fresh berries and grilled chicken.

ACTIVE TIME: 20 MINUTES · TOTAL TIME: 35 MINUTES

MAKES: 4 MAIN-DISH SERVINGS

- 2 TABLESPOONS FRESH LEMON JUICE
- 2 TABLESPOONS REDUCED-FAT SOUR CREAM
- 1 TABLESPOON HONEY
- 1 TEASPOON DIJON MUSTARD
- 3/8 TEASPOON SALT
- 3/8 TEASPOON GROUND BLACK PEPPER
- 1 TEASPOON POPPY SEEDS

- 1 POUND SKINLESS, BONELESS CHICKEN-BREAST HALVES
- 1½ TEASPOONS OLIVE OIL
- 1 AVOCADO, CUT IN HALF, PITTED BUT NOT PEELED
- 1 PINT RASPBERRIES (3 CUPS)
- 6 OUNCES MIXED GREENS
- ¼ CUP SLICED TOASTED ALMONDS

1 Prepare outdoor grill for direct grilling over medium heat.

2 In small bowl, whisk lemon juice, sour cream, honey, Dijon, and ⅛ teaspoon each salt and pepper. Stir in poppy seeds. Cover dressing; refrigerate up to 1 day.

3 With meat mallet, pound chicken to even ½-inch thickness. Rub 1 teaspoon oil over chicken; sprinkle with remaining ¼ teaspoon each salt and pepper. Rub cut sides of avocado with remaining ½ teaspoon oil. Place chicken and avocado on grill. Cook chicken 8 to 10 minutes, until instant-read thermometer inserted horizontally into thickest part of breast registers 165°F. Grill avocado 3 to 5 minutes or until grill marks appear, turning over once. Let chicken and avocado rest 5 minutes. Discard avocado peel; slice. Slice chicken.

4 In bowl, toss raspberries with 1 tablespoon dressing. In large bowl, toss greens with remaining dressing; divide among plates. Top with raspberries, chicken, avocado, and almonds.

EACH SERVING: ABOUT 300 CALORIES | 27G PROTEIN | 19G CARBOHYDRATE | 14G TOTAL FAT (3G SATURATED) | 67MG CHOLESTEROL | 320MG SODIUM ☺ ♥

CAJUN CHICKEN SALAD WITH GRAPES

Enjoy poached chicken, red pepper, and juicy grapes in a spicy, creamy dressing. We toasted the thyme and paprika to add extra flavor to the dressing and used reduced-fat sour cream to lower the fat.

ACTIVE TIME: 25 MINUTES · TOTAL TIME: 40 MINUTES
MAKES: 8 MAIN-DISH SERVINGS

1   LEMON, THINLY SLICED

1   BAY LEAF

½   TEASPOON WHOLE BLACK PEPPERCORNS

½   TEASPOON DRIED THYME

6   MEDIUM SKINLESS, BONELESS CHICKEN-BREAST HALVES (1¾ POUNDS)

¾   TEASPOON PAPRIKA

⅓   CUP LIGHT MAYONNAISE

⅓   CUP REDUCED-FAT SOUR CREAM

¾   TEASPOON SALT

¼   TEASPOON COARSELY GROUND BLACK PEPPER

⅛   TEASPOON GROUND NUTMEG

3   CUPS GREEN GRAPES (12 OUNCES), EACH CUT IN HALF

1   LARGE RED PEPPER, CUT INTO ½-INCH PIECES

½   CUP LOOSELY PACKED FRESH PARSLEY LEAVES, CHOPPED

¼   CUP THINLY SLICED RED ONION

1   LARGE PICKLED JALAPEÑO CHILE, MINCED

1   In 12-inch skillet, heat 1 *inch water* with lemon slices, bay leaf, peppercorns, and ¼ teaspoon thyme to boiling over high heat. Add chicken; reduce heat to low and simmer 12 to 14 minutes, turning chicken over halfway through cooking, until chicken just loses its pink color throughout. (An instant-read thermometer inserted horizontally into center of breast should register 165°F.) With slotted spoon or tongs, transfer chicken from skillet to cutting board; cool slightly until easy to handle. Cut chicken into ¾-inch pieces.

2   Discard poaching liquid and wipe skillet dry. Add paprika and remaining ¼ teaspoon thyme to skillet; toast over medium-low heat, stirring, 2 minutes.

3   Transfer paprika mixture to large bowl; stir in mayonnaise, sour cream, salt, black pepper, and nutmeg until blended. Add chicken, grapes, red pepper, parsley, onion, and jalapeño; toss until evenly coated. Serve salad warm, or cover and refrigerate until ready to serve.

EACH SERVING: ABOUT 200 CALORIES | 24G PROTEIN | 16G CARBOHYDRATE | 4G TOTAL FAT (1G SATURATED) | 64MG CHOLESTEROL | 380MG SODIUM ♥ ☺ ▤

TACO SALAD

Better than a taco! For quick assembly, have all the ingredients chopped and ready to go.

TOTAL TIME: 30 MINUTES

MAKES: 6 MAIN-DISH SERVINGS

- 2 TEASPOONS VEGETABLE OIL
- 1 ONION, CHOPPED
- 1 GARLIC CLOVE, FINELY CHOPPED
- 2 TABLESPOONS CHILI POWDER
- 1 TEASPOON GROUND CUMIN
- 1 POUND GROUND BEEF CHUCK
- 1 CAN (8 OUNCES) TOMATO SAUCE
- 1 HEAD ICEBERG LETTUCE, CUT INTO QUARTERS, CORED, AND VERY THINLY SLICED

- 1 LARGE RIPE TOMATO (10 OUNCES), FINELY CHOPPED
- 1 RIPE AVOCADO, PEELED, PITTED, AND CHOPPED
- 4 OUNCES SHARP CHEDDAR CHEESE, SHREDDED (1 CUP)
- 3 TABLESPOONS SOUR CREAM
- 1 CUP LOOSELY PACKED SMALL CILANTRO LEAVES
- ½ BAG (5 OUNCES) TORTILLA CHIPS

---

1 In 10-inch skillet, heat oil over medium heat. Add onion and cook, stirring occasionally, until tender, about 5 minutes. Stir in garlic, chili powder, and cumin and cook 30 seconds. Add ground beef, stirring to break up lumps with side of spoon; cook until no longer pink, about 5 minutes. Stir in tomato sauce and cook 5 minutes longer.

2 Divide lettuce among dinner plates. Spoon warm beef mixture on top of lettuce. Sprinkle with tomato, avocado, and Cheddar. Top each with some sour cream; sprinkle with cilantro. Tuck tortilla chips around edge of each plate.

TIP For a heartier dish, add drained canned beans to the beef mixture.

EACH SERVING: ABOUT 505 CALORIES | 22G PROTEIN | 21G CARBOHYDRATE | 38G TOTAL FAT (15G SATURATED) | 87MG CHOLESTEROL | 504MG SODIUM

MANGO CHICKEN LETTUCE WRAPS

Mango, mint, and jicama add Latin-American zing to these speedy, no-cook chicken wraps.

TOTAL TIME: 20 MINUTES

MAKES: 4 MAIN-DISH SERVINGS

---

1 LARGE RIPE MANGO, PEELED AND CHOPPED

1 CUP FINELY CHOPPED JICAMA

½ CUP PACKED FRESH MINT LEAVES, FINELY CHOPPED

¼ CUP FRESH LIME JUICE

2 TABLESPOONS EXTRA-VIRGIN OLIVE OIL

½ TEASPOON ASIAN CHILI SAUCE (SRIRACHA), PLUS MORE TO TASTE

¼ TEASPOON SALT

3 CUPS COARSELY SHREDDED CHICKEN MEAT (FROM ½ ROTISSERIE CHICKEN)

12 BOSTON LETTUCE LEAVES

1   In large bowl, combine mango, jicama, mint, lime juice, oil, chili sauce, and salt. Toss well. If making ahead, cover bowl and refrigerate mixture up to overnight.

2   To serve, add chicken to mango mixture; toss to combine. Place 3 lettuce leaves on each plate; divide chicken mixture equally among lettuce leaves.

EACH SERVING: ABOUT 325 CALORIES | 32G PROTEIN | 17G CARBOHYDRATE | 15G TOTAL FAT (3G SATURATED) | 94MG CHOLESTEROL | 400MG SODIUM

KOREAN STEAK IN LETTUCE CUPS

Sliced round steak and shredded carrots are sautéed in a rich soy-ginger sauce and served in delicate Boston-lettuce leaves.

TOTAL TIME: 20 MINUTES

MAKES: 4 MAIN-DISH SERVINGS

3 TABLESPOONS SOY SAUCE	4 CELERY STALKS WITH LEAVES, THINLY SLICED
1 TABLESPOON SUGAR	5 OUNCES PACKAGED SHREDDED CARROTS (1¾ CUPS)
2 TEASPOONS ASIAN SESAME OIL	
1 TEASPOON MINCED, PEELED FRESH GINGER (SEE BOX, OPPOSITE)	⅓ CUP WATER
¼ TEASPOON CAYENNE (GROUND RED) PEPPER	3 GREEN ONIONS, THINLY SLICED
	1 TABLESPOON SESAME SEEDS
1 GARLIC CLOVE, CRUSHED WITH GARLIC PRESS	1 HEAD BOSTON LETTUCE, SEPARATED INTO LEAVES
1 BEEF TOP ROUND STEAK (1 POUND), TRIMMED, CUT INTO ½-INCH CUBES	GREEN-ONION TOPS FOR GARNISH

1   In medium bowl, stir soy sauce, sugar, oil, ginger, cayenne, and garlic until blended. Add beef, turning to coat with soy-sauce mixture, and marinate 15 minutes at room temperature, stirring occasionally.

2   In 12-inch skillet, heat celery, carrots, and water to boiling over medium-high heat. Cook 2 to 3 minutes or until vegetables are tender-crisp, stirring occasionally. Add beef with its marinade and cook 2 minutes or until meat just loses its pink color throughout, stirring quickly and constantly. Stir in green onions and sesame seeds and cook 1 minute, stirring.

3   Place some beef mixture on a lettuce leaf. Garnish with green-onion tops. If you like, fold sides of lettuce leaf over filling to make a package to eat out of hand.

EACH SERVING: ABOUT 250 CALORIES | 28G PROTEIN | 12G CARBOHYDRATE | 10G TOTAL FAT (3G SATURATED) | 53MG CHOLESTEROL | 855MG SODIUM ☺ ☺

COOKING WITH FRESH GINGER

Spicy and slightly sweet, fresh ginger is widely used as an aromatic ingredient in Asian dishes. Although often called ginger root because of its appearance, it's actually a rhizome (underground stem) that contains phytonutrients, known for their powerful anti-inflammatory properties.

To peel ginger, scrape off the skin with a teaspoon, avoiding the delicate flesh underneath, which is full of flavor. Slice, chop, mince, or grate the flesh as called for in the recipe. Fresh unpeeled ginger root, tightly wrapped, can be refrigerated for up to one week or frozen for up to two months.

PHILLY CHEESE STEAKS

These sandwiches have all the flavor of the traditional Philadelphia treat but take half the time. To streamline prep, we broil the buns and beef while the onions and peppers cook on the stovetop.

TOTAL TIME: 25 MINUTES

MAKES: 4 SANDWICHES

---

1   TEASPOON OLIVE OIL

1   JUMBO ONION (12 OUNCES), THINLY SLICED

1   MEDIUM RED PEPPER, THINLY SLICED

1   MEDIUM GREEN PEPPER, THINLY SLICED

4   HERO-STYLE ROLLS (3 OUNCES EACH), CUT HORIZONTALLY IN HALF

8   OUNCES THINLY SLICED DELI ROAST BEEF

4   OUNCES THINLY SLICED PROVOLONE CHEESE

---

1   In nonstick 12-inch skillet, heat oil over medium heat until hot. Add onion and peppers and cook 12 to 15 minutes or until tender and golden, stirring occasionally.

2   Meanwhile, preheat broiler. Place rolls, cut sides up, on rack in broiling pan. Top each bottom half with one-fourth of roast beef and one-fourth of cheese. With broiling pan 5 to 7 inches from source of heat, broil 1 to 2 minutes, until cheese melts and bread is toasted.

3   Pile onion mixture on top of melted cheese; replace top halves of rolls.

EACH SANDWICH: ABOUT 620 CALORIES | 35G PROTEIN | 60G CARBOHYDRATE | 26G TOTAL FAT (12G SATURATED) | 94MG CHOLESTEROL | 500MG SODIUM

LOW 'N' SLOW PULLED PORK SANDWICHES

Preparing this dish is a breeze when you use a slow cooker. Simply combine the onion and pork with the savory sauce; set on Low and let the cooker do the rest. Serve the tangy shredded meat with soft buns for a Southern-style treat.

ACTIVE TIME: 20 MINUTES · SLOW-COOK TIME: 8 HOURS ON LOW

MAKES: 12 SANDWICHES

---

1 ONION, CHOPPED	1¼ TEASPOONS GROUND BLACK PEPPER
½ CUP KETCHUP	4 POUNDS BONELESS PORK SHOULDER BLADE ROAST (FRESH PORK BUTT), CUT INTO 4 PIECES
⅓ CUP CIDER VINEGAR	
¼ CUP PACKED BROWN SUGAR	12 SOFT SANDWICH BUNS OR CIABATTA ROLLS, WARMED
¼ CUP TOMATO PASTE	
2 TABLESPOONS SWEET PAPRIKA	DILL PICKLES, POTATO CHIPS, AND HOT SAUCE (OPTIONAL)
2 TABLESPOONS WORCESTERSHIRE SAUCE	
2 TABLESPOONS YELLOW MUSTARD	
1½ TEASPOONS SALT	

1   In 4½- to 6-quart slow-cooker pot, stir onion, ketchup, vinegar, brown sugar, tomato paste, paprika, Worcestershire, mustard, salt, and pepper until combined. Add pork to sauce mixture and turn to coat well with sauce.

2   Cover slow cooker with lid and cook on Low 8 to 10 hours or until pork is tender.

3   With tongs, transfer pork to large bowl. Turn setting to High; cover and heat sauce to boiling to thicken and reduce slightly.

4   While sauce boils, with 2 forks, pull pork into shreds. Return shredded pork to slow cooker and toss with sauce to combine. Cover slow cooker and heat through on High if necessary.

5   Spoon pork mixture onto bottom of sandwich buns; replace tops of buns. Serve with pickles, potato chips, and hot sauce if you like.

EACH SANDWICH: ABOUT 475 CALORIES | 31G PROTEIN | 29G CARBOHYDRATE | 26G TOTAL FAT (9G SATURATED) | 107MG CHOLESTEROL | 760MG SODIUM 🍴 🍲

SMOKED TURKEY AND MANGO WRAPS

A sandwich of delightful counterpoints: luscious fresh mango—underscored by mango chutney—played against the rich meatiness of smoked turkey. The sandwich components are wrapped in lahvash, the soft version of Armenian cracker bread that ranges from 9 to 16 inches in diameter. If you can't find lahvash, divide filling ingredients among four 8- to 10-inch flour tortillas.

TOTAL TIME: 25 MINUTES PLUS CHILLING

MAKES: 4 SANDWICHES

1   LARGE LIME

¼   CUP LIGHT MAYONNAISE

3   TABLESPOONS MANGO CHUTNEY, CHOPPED

½   TEASPOON CURRY POWDER

⅛   TEASPOON PAPRIKA

1   LAHVASH (HALF 14-OUNCE PACKAGE SOFT ARMENIAN FLATBREAD; SEE TIP)

1   MEDIUM CUCUMBER, PEELED AND THINLY SLICED

8   OUNCES THINLY SLICED SMOKED TURKEY BREAST

1   MEDIUM MANGO, PEELED AND FINELY CHOPPED (SEE BOX, OPPOSITE)

6   LARGE GREEN-LEAF LETTUCE LEAVES

1   Grate ¼ teaspoon peel and squeeze 1 tablespoon juice from lime. In bowl, mix lime peel and juice, mayonnaise, chutney, curry, and paprika.

2   Unfold lahvash; spread with mayonnaise mixture. Top with cucumber slices, turkey, mango, and lettuce. Roll lahvash jelly-roll fashion.

3   Wrap lahvash roll in plastic and refrigerate 2 to 4 hours to allow bread to soften and flavor to develop.

4   To serve, trim ends, then cut lahvash roll into 4 equal pieces.

TIP   If lahvash seems dry before filling, place between dampened paper towels 10 to 15 minutes to soften.

EACH SANDWICH: ABOUT 280 CALORIES | 18G PROTEIN | 51G CARBOHYDRATE | 2G TOTAL FAT (0G SATURATED) | 23MG CHOLESTEROL | 860MG SODIUM ☺ 🍽

CUTTING A MANGO

Choose a plump fruit with a fresh, sweet aroma. Ripe mangoes yield to gentle pressure. Avoid oversoft, shriveled, or bruised fruit.

With a sharp knife, cut a lengthwise slice from each side of the long flat seed, as close to the seed as possible. Peel seed section; cut off as much flesh as you can and discard seed.

Cut the mango pieces lengthwise into wedges. Use a sharp knife to remove the peel from each wedge, cutting close to the peel. Chop each slice into pieces as called for in the recipe.

TURKEY AND SPICY HUMMUS CLUBS

Adding sriracha sauce to hummus makes an easy, spicy condiment, one that pairs perfectly with this turkey club. For photo, see page 124.

TOTAL TIME: 20 MINUTES

MAKES: 4 MAIN-DISH SERVINGS

---

1 CONTAINER (8 TO 10 OUNCES) HUMMUS

1 TABLESPOON ASIAN CHILI SAUCE, LIKE SRIRACHA

¼ CUP LIGHT MAYONNAISE

¼ TEASPOON SMOKED PAPRIKA

8 SLICES REDUCED-SODIUM BACON

12 SLICES MULTIGRAIN BREAD, LIGHTLY TOASTED

8 OUNCES REDUCED-SODIUM DELI SMOKED TURKEY, THINLY SLICED

2 CUPS ARUGULA

2 MEDIUM TOMATOES, SLICED

1 In small bowl, stir together hummus and chili sauce. In another small bowl, stir together mayonnaise and smoked paprika.

2 Place 4 slices bacon on paper-towel-lined microwave-safe plate. Cover with another paper towel. Microwave on High 3 to 4 minutes or until crisp. Repeat with remaining 4 slices bacon and clean paper towels. Let cool completely; crumble.

3 Spread 1 tablespoon mayonnaise on one side of 4 slices bread. Spread 2 tablespoons hummus on one side of remaining slices of bread.

4 For each sandwich: Place one-fourth of turkey on 1 slice of bread with hummus. Place bread with mayonnaise on top, face up. Layer 2 slices bacon, one-fourth of arugula, and one-fourth of tomatoes on top of mayo. Top with another slice of bread with hummus.

EACH SERVING: ABOUT 585 CALORIES | 35G PROTEIN | 60G CARBOHYDRATE | 25G TOTAL FAT (3G SATURATED) | 53MG CHOLESTEROL | 1,500MG SODIUM ✓

CHICKEN CAESAR POCKETS

A sandwich and a salad rolled into one, these pockets make great picnic fare. Of course, you can always skip the pita and serve the salad on its own.

ACTIVE TIME: 15 MINUTES · TOTAL TIME: 25 MINUTES

MAKES: 6 SANDWICHES

¼ TEASPOON SALT	1 TABLESPOON DIJON MUSTARD
2 TEASPOONS PLUS 3 TABLESPOONS OLIVE OIL	1 TEASPOON ANCHOVY PASTE
½ TEASPOON COARSELY GROUND BLACK PEPPER	1 SMALL GARLIC CLOVE, CRUSHED WITH GARLIC PRESS
4 MEDIUM SKINLESS, BONELESS CHICKEN-BREAST HALVES (1 POUND)	½ CUP GRATED PARMESAN CHEESE
3 TABLESPOONS LEMON JUICE	6 PITAS (6- TO 7-INCH DIAMETER)
3 TABLESPOONS LIGHT MAYONNAISE	8 CUPS SLICED ROMAINE LETTUCE (FROM ONE 12-OUNCE HEAD)

1 Preheat broiler. In medium bowl, mix salt, 2 teaspoons oil, and ¼ teaspoon pepper. Add chicken and stir to coat. Place chicken on rack in broiling pan. Place pan in broiler at closest position to source of heat; broil chicken about 12 minutes, turning once, until juices run clear when thickest part is pierced with tip of knife. (An instant-read thermometer inserted horizontally into center of breast should register 165°F.) Transfer chicken to cutting board; cool 5 minutes or until chicken is easy to handle.

2 Meanwhile, in large bowl, with fork, mix lemon juice, mayonnaise, mustard, anchovy paste, garlic, remaining 3 tablespoons oil, and ¼ teaspoon pepper until blended; stir in Parmesan.

3 With sharp knife, slit top third of each pita to form an opening. Thinly slice chicken. Add lettuce and chicken slices to dressing; toss well to coat. Fill pitas with salad.

EACH SANDWICH: ABOUT 345 CALORIES | 17G PROTEIN | 39G CARBOHYDRATE | 13G TOTAL FAT (3G SATURATED) | 26MG CHOLESTEROL | 770MG SODIUM ✓ ☺

A TRIO OF TARTINES

These easy-to-assemble open-faced sandwiches are the best thing since sliced bread. Try the Roast Beef and Relish Tartines, which elevate the ordinary roast beef sandwich, or dress up your usual lunch-time sandwich with a luscious crab salad. For a more gourmet take on cream cheese and lox, try the salmon, crumbled goat cheese, and tomato option.

CRAB SALAD TOASTS

TOTAL TIME: 15 MINUTES

MAKES: 4 MAIN-DISH SERVINGS

1   LEMON

¼   CUP NONFAT GREEK YOGURT

2   TABLESPOONS LIGHT MAYONNAISE

2   TEASPOONS DIJON MUSTARD

1   SMALL GARLIC CLOVE, CRUSHED WITH GARLIC PRESS

¼   TEASPOON OLD BAY SEASONING

¼   TEASPOON SALT

¼   TEASPOON FRESHLY GROUND BLACK PEPPER

8   OUNCES COOKED LUMP CRABMEAT, PICKED OVER

2   LARGE STALKS CELERY, FINELY CHOPPED

1   SMALL GRANNY SMITH APPLE, CORED AND FINELY CHOPPED

2   TEASPOONS SNIPPED CHIVES, PLUS MORE FOR GARNISH

4   SLICES (ABOUT 7 INCHES WIDE) COUNTRY WHITE BREAD, OR 8 SMALL SLICES, LIGHTLY TOASTED

Into large bowl, from lemon, grate 1 teaspoon peel and squeeze 1 tablespoon juice. Add yogurt, mayonnaise, mustard, garlic, Old Bay seasoning, salt, and pepper; stir to combine. To same bowl, add crab, celery, and apple; stir to combine. Fold in chives. Divide among bread slices. Garnish with additional chives if desired.

EACH SERVING: ABOUT 220 CALORIES | 15G PROTEIN | 29G CARBOHYDRATE | 5G TOTAL FAT (1G SATURATED) | 58MG CHOLESTEROL | 765MG SODIUM 😊 ☺

SMOKED SALMON TARTINES

TOTAL TIME: 20 MINUTES

MAKES: 4 MAIN-DISH SERVINGS

¼ CUP RED WINE VINEGAR

2 TABLESPOONS WATER

2 TEASPOONS SUGAR

PINCH OF SALT

2 SHALLOTS, VERY THINLY SLICED

4 OUNCES CREAM CHEESE, SOFTENED

4 LARGE SLICES PUMPERNICKEL BREAD, LIGHTLY TOASTED

3 PLUM TOMATOES, THINLY SLICED

8 OUNCES SMOKED SALMON, SLICED

1 OUNCE GOAT CHEESE, CRUMBLED

½ CUP WATERCRESS, TRIMMED

In small microwave-safe bowl, mix vinegar, water, sugar, and salt. Add shallots, stirring to combine. Microwave on High 2 to 3 minutes; drain and let cool. Spread cream cheese on each slice of bread. Layer each with tomatoes, salmon, and shallots. Top with goat cheese and watercress.

EACH SERVING: ABOUT 310 CALORIES | 18G PROTEIN | 26G CARBOHYDRATE | 15G TOTAL FAT (8G SATURATED) | 48MG CHOLESTEROL | 890MG SODIUM ♥ ☺

ROAST BEEF AND RELISH TARTINES

TOTAL TIME: 20 MINUTES

MAKES: 4 MAIN-DISH SERVINGS

¼ CUP SOUR CREAM

1 TEASPOON DRAINED PREPARED HORSERADISH

½ CUP FINELY CHOPPED ROASTED RED PEPPER

¼ CUP SWEET RELISH

4 LARGE SLICES SOURDOUGH BREAD (½ INCH THICK), TOASTED

12 OUNCES DELI ROAST BEEF, THINLY SLICED

SALT AND FRESHLY GROUND BLACK PEPPER (OPTIONAL)

¼ SMALL SEEDLESS (ENGLISH) CUCUMBER, THINLY SLICED AT AN ANGLE

½ CUP CHOPPED FRISÉE LETTUCE

In small bowl, mix sour cream and horseradish. In another small bowl, mix red pepper and relish. Spread sour cream mixture on each slice of bread. Layer each with roast beef and season with pinch each salt and pepper if desired. Top with pepper relish, then cucumber slices and frisée.

EACH SERVING: ABOUT 280 CALORIES | 27G PROTEIN | 29G CARBOHYDRATE | 7G TOTAL FAT (3G SATURATED) | 51MG CHOLESTEROL | 585MG SODIUM ♥ ☺

MUFFULETTAS

This sandwich was born in the French Quarter of New Orleans, but with our recipe you won't have to travel to get it. It tastes best when refrigerated for a few hours after assembly to allow the flavors to meld together.

TOTAL TIME: 25 MINUTES

MAKES: 4 MAIN-DISH SERVINGS

1 CUP GIARDINIERA (SEE TIP), RINSED, DRAINED, AND ROUGHLY CHOPPED

¼ CUP PIMIENTO-STUFFED OLIVES, RINSED, DRAINED, AND SLICED

¼ CUP PEPPERONCINI, RINSED, DRAINED, AND SLICED

2 STALKS CELERY, THINLY SLICED AT AN ANGLE

¼ CUP PACKED FRESH FLAT-LEAF PARSLEY LEAVES

2 TABLESPOONS EXTRA-VIRGIN OLIVE OIL

⅛ TEASPOON FRESHLY GROUND BLACK PEPPER

1 LOAF (8-INCH ROUND) ARTISANAL COUNTRY BREAD

4 OUNCES GENOA SALAMI, THINLY SLICED

4 OUNCES LOWER-SODIUM DELI HAM, THINLY SLICED

4 OUNCES PROVOLONE CHEESE, THINLY SLICED

1   In large bowl, combine giardiniera, olives, pepperoncini, celery, parsley, 1 tablespoon oil, and pepper. Toss until well mixed.

2   Use serrated knife to cut bread in half horizontally. With fingers, remove most of center of bread, leaving 1 inch of bread all around crust. Reserve center of bread for another use.

3   Drizzle 1 tablespoon oil all over cut sides of loaf. Layer salami and ham on bottom half of bread. Top with giardiniera mixture, then cheese. Cover with top half of bread, pressing top down. Use serrated knife to cut sandwich into quarters. Sandwiches can be wrapped tightly and refrigerated up to 1 day.

TIP Giardiniera—an Italian ready-made mix of pickled veggies—adds tons of flavor fast.

EACH SERVING: ABOUT 385 CALORIES | 20G PROTEIN | 16G CARBOHYDRATE | 26G TOTAL FAT (9G SATURATED) | 61MG CHOLESTEROL | 1,600MG SODIUM

FALAFEL SANDWICHES

Serve these Middle Eastern chickpea patties the traditional way—in pita pockets with lettuce, tomatoes, and cucumbers. For a tangy finishing touch, spoon in a little plain yogurt.

TOTAL TIME: 30 MINUTES

MAKES: 4 SANDWICHES

4   GREEN ONIONS, CUT INTO 1-INCH PIECES

2   GARLIC CLOVES, EACH CUT IN HALF

½   CUP PACKED FRESH ITALIAN PARSLEY LEAVES

2   TEASPOONS DRIED MINT

1   CAN (15 TO 19 OUNCES) GARBANZO BEANS, RINSED AND DRAINED

½   CUP PLAIN DRIED BREAD CRUMBS

1   TEASPOON GROUND CORIANDER

1   TEASPOON GROUND CUMIN

1   TEASPOON BAKING POWDER

½   TEASPOON SALT

¼   TEASPOON CAYENNE (GROUND RED) PEPPER

¼   TEASPOON GROUND ALLSPICE

OLIVE OIL NONSTICK COOKING SPRAY

4   PITAS (6- TO 7-INCH DIAMETER)

ACCOMPANIMENTS: SLICED ROMAINE LETTUCE, SLICED TOMATOES, SLICED CUCUMBER, SLICED RED ONION, PLAIN LOW-FAT YOGURT

1   In food processor with knife blade attached, finely chop green onions, garlic, parsley, and mint. Add garbanzo beans, bread crumbs, coriander, cumin, baking powder, salt, cayenne, and allspice and blend until a coarse puree forms.

2   Shape bean mixture, by scant ½ cups, into eight 3-inch round patties; place on sheet of waxed paper. Spray both sides of patties with olive oil cooking spray.

3   Heat nonstick 10-inch skillet over medium heat until hot. Add half of patties and cook 8 to 10 minutes or until dark golden brown, turning once. Transfer patties to paper towels to drain. Repeat with remaining patties.

4   Cut off top third of each pita to form a pocket. Place warm patties in pitas. Serve with choice of accompaniments.

EACH SANDWICH: ABOUT 365 CALORIES | 14G PROTEIN | 68G CARBOHYDRATE | 5G TOTAL FAT (1G SATURATED) | 0MG CHOLESTEROL | 1,015MG SODIUM

PINTO-BEAN BURGERS

These zesty burgers are a family-friendly solution when you need to have dinner on the table fast.

ACTIVE TIME: 15 MINUTES · TOTAL TIME: 25 MINUTES

MAKES: 4 BURGERS

1   CAN (15 TO 19 OUNCES) PINTO BEANS, RINSED AND DRAINED

1   TEASPOON GROUND CUMIN

1   TEASPOON MINCED CANNED CHIPOTLE CHILE IN ADOBO

1   SLICE PICKLED JALAPEÑO CHILE, MINCED

2   TABLESPOONS PLUS ½ CUP MILD SALSA

5   TABLESPOONS PLAIN DRIED BREAD CRUMBS

2   TABLESPOONS OLIVE OIL

4   HAMBURGER BUNS, WARMED

4   LETTUCE LEAVES

ACCOMPANIMENTS: CILANTRO LEAVES, SLICED RED ONION, SOUR CREAM (OPTIONAL)

1   In medium bowl, with potato masher, mash pinto beans until almost smooth. Stir in cumin, chipotle, jalapeño, 2 tablespoons salsa, and 2 tablespoons bread crumbs until combined.

2   Place remaining 3 tablespoons bread crumbs on sheet of waxed paper. With floured hands, shape bean mixture into four 3-inch round patties; coat evenly with bread crumbs.

3   In nonstick 12-inch skillet, heat oil over medium heat until hot. Add burgers and cook until lightly browned and heated through, about 8 minutes, turning over once.

4   Spoon remaining ½ cup salsa on bottom halves of buns; top with lettuce and burgers. Serve with cilantro, red onion, and sour cream if you like.

EACH BURGER: ABOUT 350 CALORIES | 11G PROTEIN | 51G CARBOHYDRATE | 11G TOTAL FAT (2G SATURATED) | 0MG CHOLESTEROL | 775MG SODIUM

GENERAL INDEX

Note: Page numbers in **bold** indicate recipe category summaries/overviews.

INDEX OF RECIPES BY ICON

This index makes it easy to search recipes by category, including 30 minutes or less, heart-healthy, low-calorie, make-ahead, and slow-cooker dishes.

◔ 30 MINUTES OR LESS

These easy weekday meals and treats are perfect for busy home cooks. Each require 30 minutes or less to prepare—from kitchen to table!

♥ HEART HEALTHY

If you're looking for heart-healthy options, look no further. Each main dish contains 5 grams or less saturated fat, 150 milligrams or less cholesterol, and 480 milligrams or less sodium.

☺ LOW CALORIE

This list will come in handy if you're keeping track of your daily caloric intake. Main-dish meals (which include a starch or fruit) that are 450 calories or less per serving are included, along with all other main dishes that are 300 calories or less per serving.

🍴 MAKE AHEAD

For convenience, you can make all (or a portion) of these recipes ahead of time. The individual recipes indicate which steps you can do-ahead or how long you can refrigerate or freeze the completed dish.

🍲 SLOW COOKER

These slow-cooked dishes make it easy to get dinner on the table. Just put all the ingredients in the bowl of your slow cooker in the A.M., and you'll have a delicious, ready-to-serve main dish in the P.M.

PHOTOGRAPHY CREDITS

James Baigrie: 14, 22, 28, 94
Renée Comet: 11
Getty Images: David Bishop Inc., 101
Brian Hagiwara: 58, 87, 91, 99, 104, 113, 127
iStockphoto: ALEAIMAGE, 115; Kaan Ates, 56; Maria Brzostowska, 109 top; Le Do, 129; Kevin Dyer, 59; James Harrop, 138; Tobias Helbig, 89; Sylwia Kachel, 53; Sarah Lee, 77; Milos Luzanin, 103; Natikka, 141; Vitalina Rybakova, 70; Alina Solovyova-Vincent, 109 bottom; George Tsartsianidis, 39; YinYang, 109 middle; Feng Yu, 63
Rita Maas: 41, 61
Kate Mathis: 13, 36, 42, 110, 116, 130, 135
Ngoc Minh Ngo: 50
Con Poulos: 6, 66, 69, 73, 75, 78, 82, 107, 124, 146
Alan Richardson: 18, 137
Kate Sears: 2
Ann Stratton: 47
Studio D: Philip Friedman, 7, 8, 10, 27; J Muckle, 97
Mark Thomas: 25, 64, 81, 119, 123
Anna Williams: 33, 55

Front Cover: James Baigrie
Spine: Kate Mathis
Back Cover (all): Con Poulos

METRIC EQUIVALENTS

The recipes that appear in this cookbook use the standard United States method for measuring liquid and dry or solid ingredients (teaspoons, tablespoons, and cups). The information on this chart is provided to help cooks outside the U.S. successfully use these recipes. All equivalents are approximate.

METRIC EQUIVALENTS FOR DIFFERENT TYPES OF INGREDIENTS
A standard cup measure of a dry or solid ingredient will vary in weight depending on the type of ingredient. A standard cup of liquid is the same volume for any type of liquid. Use the following chart when converting standard cup measures to grams (weight) or milliliters (volume).

Standard Cup	Fine Powder (e.g. flour)	Grain (e.g. rice)	Granular (e.g. sugar)	Liquid Solids (e.g. butter)	Liquid (e.g. milk)
1	140 g	150 g	190 g	200 g	240 ml
¾	105 g	113 g	143 g	150 g	180 ml
⅔	93 g	100 g	125 g	133 g	160 ml
½	70 g	75 g	95 g	100 g	120 ml
⅓	47 g	50 g	63 g	67 g	80 ml
¼	35 g	38 g	48 g	50 g	60 ml
⅛	18 g	19 g	24 g	25 g	30 ml

USEFUL EQUIVALENTS FOR LIQUID INGREDIENTS BY VOLUME

¼ tsp	=					1 ml
½ tsp	=					2 ml
1 tsp	=					5 ml
3 tsp	=	1 tbls	=		½ fl oz	=	15 ml
		2 tbls	=	⅛ cup	=	1 fl oz	=	30 ml
		4 tbls	=	¼ cup	=	2 fl oz	=	60 ml
		5⅓ tbls	=	⅓ cup	=	3 fl oz	=	80 ml
		8 tbls	=	½ cup	=	4 fl oz	=	120 ml
		10⅔ tbls	=	⅔ cup	=	5 fl oz	=	160 ml
		12 tbls	=	¾ cup	=	6 fl oz	=	180 ml
		16 tbls	=	1 cup	=	8 fl oz	=	240 ml
		1 pt	=	2 cups	=	16 fl oz	=	480 ml
		1 qt	=	4 cups	=	32 fl oz	=	960 ml
						33 fl oz	= 1000 ml	= 1 L

USEFUL EQUIVALENTS FOR COOKING/OVEN TEMPERATURES

	Fahrenheit	Celsius	Gas Mark
Freeze Water	32° F	0° C	
Room Temperature	68° F	20° C	
Boil Water	212° F	100° C	
Bake	325° F	160° C	3
	350° F	180° C	4
	375° F	190° C	5
	400° F	200° C	6
	425° F	220° C	7
	450° F	230° C	8
Broil			Grill

USEFUL EQUIVALENTS FOR DRY INGREDIENTS BY WEIGHT
(To convert ounces to grams, multiply the number of ounces by 30.)

1 oz	=	¹⁄₁₆ lb	=	30 g
2 oz	=	¼ lb	=	120 g
4 oz	=	½ lb	=	240 g
8 oz	=	¾ lb	=	360 g
16 oz	=	1 lb	=	480 g

USEFUL EQUIVALENTS LENGTH
(To convert inches to centimeters, multiply the number of inches by 2.5.)

1 in	=		2.5 cm
6 in	=	½ ft =	15 cm
12 in	=	1 ft =	30 cm
36 in	=	3 ft = 1 yd	= 90 cm
40 in	=		100 cm = 1 m

THE GOOD HOUSEKEEPING TRIPLE-TEST PROMISE

At *Good Housekeeping*, we want to make sure that every recipe we print works in any oven, with any brand of ingredient, no matter what. That's why, in our test kitchens at the **Good Housekeeping Research Institute,** we go all out: We test each recipe at least three times—and, often, several more times after that.

When a recipe is first developed, one member of our team prepares the dish and we judge it on these criteria: It must be **delicious, family-friendly, healthy,** and **easy to make.**

1 The recipe is then tested several more times to fine-tune the flavor and ease of preparation, always by the same team member, using the same equipment.

2 Next, another team member follows the recipe as written, **varying the brands of ingredients** and **kinds of equipment.** Even the types of stoves we use are changed.

3 A third team member repeats the whole process **using yet another set of equipment** and **alternative ingredients.** By the time the recipes appear on these pages, they are guaranteed to work in any kitchen, including yours. **WE PROMISE.**